I0450260

Developmental Social Work in Disability Issues:

Research and Practice for Promoting
Participation in Rural Sri Lanka

Developmental Social Work in Disability Issues:

Research and Practice for Promoting
Participation in Rural Sri Lanka

Masateru Higashida

Ashoka Disability Research Forum

2019

First Published 2019

by Ashoka Disability Research Forum

12, Ikeda-cho, Nishinomiya-shi, Hyogo, Japan 6620911

http://www.lulu.com/spotlight/ashoka

Simultaneously published

by Glasstree Academic Publishing

https://glasstree.com/shop/

Copyright © 2019 by Masateru Higashida

All rights reserved. This book or any portion thereof may not be reproduced or used in any manner whatsoever without the express written permission of the publisher except for the use of brief quotations in a book review or scholarly journal.

ISBN 978-0-359-49868-0

DOI:10.20850/9781534299863

To my wife

Contents

ACKNOWLEDGEMENTS

I would like to start by expressing my gratitude to all of the disabled people and their family members who participated in our research project in Sri Lanka. This book would not have been possible without your precious participation.

I am very grateful to staff members of the Department of Social Services in Sri Lanka, Vanni Rehabilitation Organization for the Differently-Abled (VAROD), as well as the Japan International Cooperation Agency (JICA) for setting up the placement and supporting this research. I am grateful to the academic staff of the National Institute of Social Development for providing valuable information. I would also like to thank the staff members in Divisional Secretariats and non-government organisations for supporting this project.

In addition, I would like to express my sincere gratitude to my supervisor, Dr Masato Kawamori of Osaka University, for your academic support and suggestions.

PREFACE

The initial concept of this book was a result of my personal experiences as an international social worker in rural areas of Sri Lanka. After working as a social worker in mental health and disability issues for approximately seven years in Japan, I was dispatched to Sri Lanka by the Japan International Cooperation Agency (JICA) for two years in January 2013—this was the first trip to the country. I was in charge of social work in the community-based rehabilitation (CBR) programme. Since then, I have also conducted research in cooperation with local stakeholders in Sri Lanka, whilst coming and going between the two countries. This book is based on the research and practical findings that I extracted from my published articles.

Through the research and practice, together with my residential experiences in Sri Lanka, I have learned a great deal from disabled people and local people working at the grassroots level. I have also exchanged ideas with local and international stakeholders through meeting, trainings, events, and some other opportunities. I subsequently realised that the practical approach used in rural Sri Lanka by frontline officers in their work with disabled people would be useful for social work practitioners and researchers in other developing countries. I hope that this book contributes to realisation of the empowerment of disabled people and the disability-inclusive society.

Many disabled people in fact have experienced exclusion from the mainstream, particularly in developing countries, which has left them with limited opportunities to participate in society. The World Health

Organization (WHO) has promoted CBR since the end of the 1970s to address these global disability issues, including limited opportunities for socioeconomic participation of disabled people. Sri Lanka commenced the pilot CBR project in the dawning age of CBR, upgrading it to a national programme in the early 1990s. Frontline workers such as social services officers in the public sector and workers in NGOs are in charge of CBR to promote the empowerment and participation of disabled people at the grassroots level. However, the literature is limited in terms of the status of socioeconomic participation by disabled people and the practical skills and approaches of frontline workers—many of whom are para-professional or non-professional—to promote the participation.

This book aims to examine the socioeconomic participation of disabled people in rural Sri Lanka to explore practical strategies for promoting their participation from the perspective of developmental social work. Before examining the issues, the concepts of socioeconomic participation as a theoretical framework and developmental social work as a practical framework are discussed using the capability approach. In terms of the practical framework, I argue that the developmental social work perspective is practically useful for frontline workers to promote the socioeconomic participation of disabled people. Their practices include social investment strategies, developing resources, changing environmental factors, and promoting the self-determination of disabled people to expand opportunities for socioeconomic participation. I also highlight the necessity of a context-specific perspective such as collecting information on the values (i.e., what opportunities for participation should be included) expressed by disabled people through dialogue.

Based on these theoretical and practical frameworks, together with policy analysis of Sri Lankan CBR, the field research was undertaken collaboratively with local stakeholders in three districts: Gampaha,

Mullaitivu, and Anuradhapura. The project used a mixed-methods approach—a quantitative survey and a qualitative study—to investigate practices in rural community settings in order to analyse various data and expand the range of data analysis. First, the three placement areas were compared through a situation analysis of the socioeconomic participation of disabled people. Second, the factors associated with socioeconomic participation were analysed. Third, developmental social work practices to promote socioeconomic participation were then examined in the CBR model area.

Although this book is not comprehensive and it is far from perfect, I attempted to verify the status of the socioeconomic participation of disabled people and practical strategies. The developmental social work practices by frontline workers in Sri Lanka included an indigenous approach, a comprehensive and multisectoral approach, and social investment strategies. I argued that their practices could change environmental factors, develop community resources, and expand opportunities for the socioeconomic participation of disabled people.

This book is based on findings from just one case country, but readers could develop and apply the ideas contained in this book because of its in-depth analysis. First, some readers may be interested in the approach and concrete activities of developmental social work that could be appropriable to other contexts. Second, some readers may apply the perspective of context-specific and indigenous practices in other regions. Third, other readers may pay attention to the integration of research and practice with my different positionality in each field, although I would not use the term 'action research' in this book.

Regardless of the aspects to which one's attention is drawn, I hope that this book will give some sort of inspiration and ideas to readers and will contribute to other fields. Personally, I would also like to make use of the experiences and findings in other contexts, including Mongolia where I am working as a JICA expert in the technical cooperation project for promoting social participation of persons with disabilities in Ulaanbaatar.

I would like to express my deepest and heartfelt condolences to the people of Sri Lanka and all those affected by Easter bombings on the 21ˢᵗ April 2019.

Masateru Higashida in Mongolia, April 2019

ACRONYMS AND ABBREVIATIONS

AKASA	Association of Women with Disabilities
CBID	Community-Based Inclusive Development
CBR	Community-Based Rehabilitation
CRCs	Community Rehabilitation Committees
CRPD	Convention on the Rights of Persons with Disabilities
DCS	Department of Census and Statistics
DPOs	Disabled People's Organisations
DS	Divisional Secretariat
ESCAP	Economic and Social Commission for Asia and the Pacific
HDI	Human Development Index
ICF	International Classification of Functioning, Disability and Health
JOCVs	Japan Overseas Cooperation Volunteers
JSWs	Japanese Social Workers
LTTE	Liberation Tigers of Tamil Eelam
MOH	Medical Officer of Health
MSS	Ministry of Social Services
NISD	National Institute of Social Development
RS	Religion and Spirituality
Rs.	Sri Lankan Rupees
SDGs	Sustainable Development Goals

SSO	Social Services Officer
UN	United Nations
UNESCO	United Nations Educational, Scientific and Cultural Organization
UNICEF	United Nations Children's Fund/United Nations Children's Emergency Fund
VAROD	Vanni Rehabilitation Organization for the Differently-Abled
WHO	World Health Organization
WHO-DAS-II	World Health Organization disability assessment schedule (version 2.0)
YSO	Youth Services Officer

TERMINOLOGY

Developmental social work:

This is a holistic approach to addressing poverty alleviation and social inclusion, recognising the link between social and economic development, and construing welfare as an investment in human capital rather than as a drain on limited resources (Elliott & Mayadas 2001; Gray, 2002; Knapp & Midgley, 2010; Midgley, 2010). This book uses the term '(developmental) social worker(s)' to refer to anyone who performs the substantive functions of developmental social work (cf. Akimoto, 2017). The fact is that, despite lacking professional qualifications, there are many social workers and frontline workers who tackle social and developmental issues in developing countries, including Sri Lanka (See Sections 1.3. and 2.1.).

Disability:

The term is defined differently depending on the perspectives of various models of disability (See Sections 1.2 and 1.4). For example, the capability approach and the human development model regard disability as deprived capabilities and functionings amongst persons with health deprivations, which also interact with other factors (Terzi, 2005; Mitra, 2006, 2017). Although this book considers the capability approach, the research in this book (Chapters 2 to 9) also refers, for exploring the representation of disability, to the concepts and statistical data that Sri Lankan stakeholders use.

The term 'disabled people'— instead of 'people with disabilities'—is used in this book, except for cited description. As Carr and Darke (2012) argue, 'the term "people with disabilities" …is inaccurate, individualistic and it blurs the key distinction between impairment/disability…Society disables people by creating or approving barriers to their inclusion or participation' (p.59).

Socioeconomic participation:

The meaning of the terms 'social participation' or 'socioeconomic participation' appears to be broad and occasionally vague in the literature. With regard to the community-level socioeconomic participation of disabled people who are at a productive age, this concept would be interchangeable to some extent with the terms 'community participation' and 'social participation' due to potentially overlapping activities. In order to show the range of discussions about this concept, this book temporarily adapts Chang et al.'s (2013: p.772) definition of community participation to broadly define the socioeconomic participation of those who are at a productive age as 'pro-active involvement in activities that are intrinsically socioeconomic and occur either outside the home or as part of a non-domestic role' (See Section 1.2.).

Community-based rehabilitation (CBR):

As 'concern with the use of the term "rehabilitation"' was expressed in the International Consultation to Review Community-Based Rehabilitation (World Health Organization [WHO], 2003), it remains controversial whether 'rehabilitation' with a medical perspective is prioritised in CBR. Nevertheless, international organisations such as the WHO have placed CBR in the general community and social development sphere as a strategy to address disability-related inequalities and poverty, and to promote the empowerment and inclusion of disabled people. In addition, the WHO et al (2010) introduces community-based inclusive development (CBID) as the overall goal of CBR (See Section 1.1.). This book refers to CBR as a concept except where CBR denotes a specific programme, officer, or indicator.

LIST OF TABLES

LIST OF FIGURES

Map of Study Site

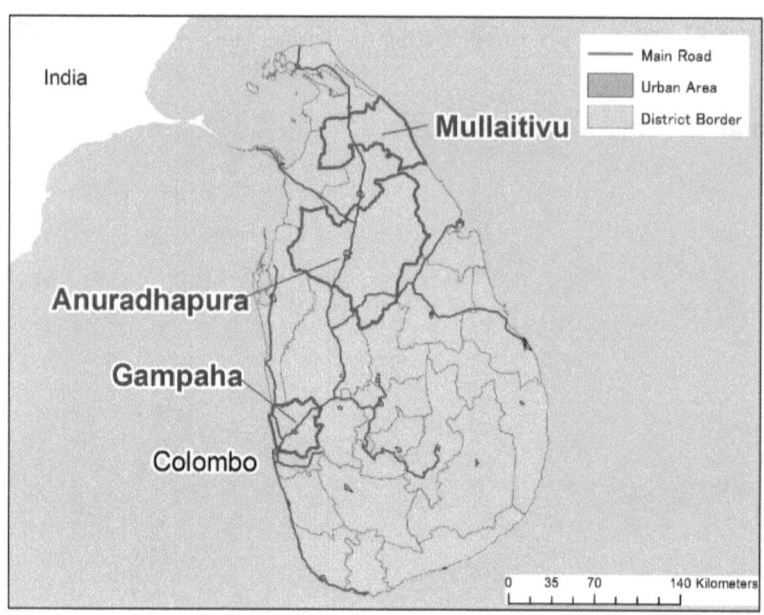

Note: Created with ArcMap10.4 by the author, using data from Esri, USGS, and NOAA.

Basic Information of Sri Lanka

Country name	Democratic Socialist Republic of Sri Lanka
Capital	Sri Jayawardenepura Kotte
Largest city	Colombo
Area	65,610 km^2
Population (estimated)	21.7million (2018)
Official languages	Sinhala and Tamil (English is a 'link language')
Ethnic group (2012)	Sinhalese (74.9%) Sri Lankan Tamils (11.2%) Sri Lankan Moors (9.2%) Indian Tamils (4.2%) Others (0.5%)
Religion (2012)	Buddhism (70.1%) Hindu (12.6%) Islam (9.7%) Christianity (7.6%)
Currency	Sri Lankan Rupee

Source of Statistics: Department of Census and Statistics (http://www.statistics.gov.lk/)

CHAPTER ONE

Introduction

(When I was on a bus) a disabled male got on.
Whilst showing traces of surgery on his chest, he
said, 'Owing to my bad health, I can no longer
work. I live with my two daughters and wife and
we are very poor...I would appreciate it if you
could donate a little bit to me. You would get
merit out of helping'. (Field diary, 21 April 2018)

The first chapter reviews current global disability issues, focusing on the restricted socioeconomic participation of disabled people in developing countries. I discuss the concept of socioeconomic participation using the capability approach. I then explore the practical framework for developmental social work in the context of community-based rehabilitation (CBR) designed to promote the socioeconomic participation of disabled people. After identifying the research gaps in disability issues in Sri Lanka, I present the overall purpose and structure of this paper.

1.1 Background: Global Disability Issues and Community-Based Rehabilitation (CBR)

This section gives a brief overview of some current worldwide situations of disability issues and CBR. I reveal that the concept of participation, including its definitions and frameworks, appears to be well-documented in disability studies and related arenas. However, I argue that disabled people, particularly in developing countries, are still likely to be excluded from society.

Global disability issues and frameworks

The global situation for disability issues has moved towards the further inclusion and empowerment of disabled people in the 21st century. The establishment of the Convention on the Rights of Persons with Disabilities (CRPD) (United Nations [UN], 2006), for example, is a significant occurrence. The CRPD, which is an international treaty of human rights, was established through the active participation of disabled people (Kayess & French, 2008); it emphasised 'full and effective participation and inclusion in society' (UN, 2006: Article 3). In addition, various stakeholders created an environment that involved disabled people in the consultation process for including disability-inclusive goals in the Sustainable Development Goals (SDGs; UN, 2018; UN

2

Partnership on the Rights of Persons with Disabilities, 2013). As a result, the SDGs include sentences related to disability in Goals 4, 8, 10, 11, and 17, whilst linking to disability-inclusive development through the use of some related-terms, such as 'inclusion', 'for all', 'accessible' and 'universal', in Goals 1, 3, 5, 9, 13 and 16 (ESCAP, 2018; UN, 2015, 2016, 2018). Thus, global actors, such as disabled people themselves and international organisations, have made efforts to promote the participation of disabled people in society, including in decision-making processes.

Disabled people, however, have historically been excluded from mainstream society (Oliver & Barnes, 1998), particularly in the global South (Klasing, 2007; Meekosha, 2011), resulting in their limited participation in the community. About 15% of the world's population is estimated to be disabled (World Bank & World Health Organization [WHO], 2011), whilst about 80% of disabled people live in developing countries (UN, 2006). Only 5% of disabled children receive an education in member states of the Economic and Social Commission for Asia and the Pacific (ESCAP, 1993); 80–90% of disabled people may be unemployed; and 80% of disabilities may result from poverty (Bieler, 2006). Therefore, the vicious cycle of social exclusion, limited opportunities for participation, and poverty exacerbates the lives of disabled people and should be addressed all over the world: reducing such downside risks is the important priority in disability issues.

Community-based rehabilitation and inclusive development as global strategies

Frameworks for global disability and health issues—in particular, CBR and community-based inclusive development (CBID)—are useful when considering entry points for promoting the participation of disabled people in practice. Indeed, many countries and organisations apply these frameworks to policies and programmes.

Table 1 shows the world progress towards full participation for disabled people. Global actors, such as the WHO, conceptualised CBR in the late 1970s, when primary health care (PHC) was declared in Alma-Ata (WHO & UN Children's Emergency Fund [UNICEF], 1978). CBR is defined as 'a strategy within general community development for the rehabilitation, equalization of opportunities, and social inclusion of all people with disabilities' (International Labour Organization [ILO] et al., 2004: p.2). The strategies and concepts of CBR and PHC have been developed by taking full advantage of synergies. The CBR matrix that was proposed by the WHO et al. (2010) identifies five domains, namely 'health', 'education', 'livelihood', 'social', and 'empowerment' (Figure 1). CBR has been further developed as CBID (WHO et al., 2010), emphasising the importance of comprehensive and disability-inclusive development as a general theme. The domains of inclusiveness are not limited to health, social services, and education, but should also include earning a living and socioeconomic development.

The model practices and evidence of the effects of the global strategy, including the standardised guidelines (WHO et al., 2010), are well-demonstrated in the literature (e.g., Cayetano & Elkins 2016; Lukersmith et al., 2013; Mauro et al., 2014, 2015; Mitchell, 1999). The CBR guidelines (WHO et al., 2010) suggest the following management cycle of CBR for stakeholders, such as project managers: situation analysis (Stage 1), planning and design (Stage 2), implementation and monitoring (Stage 3), and evaluation (Stage 4).

Table 1: Brief history of development of CBR

Year	Event	Notes
1968	'Where There Is No Doctor' by Werner, D. et al.	A model of community-based healthcare was shown.
1975	Declaration on the Rights of Disabled Persons	
1978	Declaration of Alma-Ata	The first global declaration of primary health care that had impacts on development of CBR.
1979	'Training in the Community for People with Disabilities' published by the WHO	The first CBR manual by the WHO.
1981	International Year of Disabled Persons (IYDP) by the UN	
1983–92	United Nations Decade of Disabled Persons 1983–1992 World Programme of Action Concerning Disabled Persons	Includes recommendation for promotion of CBR.
1989	'Training in the Community for People with Disabilities' published by the WHO	The revised CBR manual.
1994	Joint Position Paper by ILO, UNESCO, WHO	Clarification of definition, purpose, and methods of CBR.
2000–15	Millennium Development Goals (MDGs)	Disability-related goals are not mentioned specifically.
2004	Joint Position Paper by ILO, UNESCO, WHO (Revised version)	Human rights, poverty reduction, and inclusion are emphasised.
2006	Convention on the Rights of Persons with Disabilities	
2009	Realizing the Millennium Development Goals for persons with disabilities towards 2015 and beyond	UN General Assembly Resolution.
2010	Community-based rehabilitation guidelines (with CBR matrix)	Clarification of community-based inclusive development (CBID).
2011	World Report on Disability	
2014–21	WHO global disability action plan 2014–2021	
2015	Community-based rehabilitation indicators introduced by the WHO	
2015–30	Sustainable Development Goals (SDGs)	Disability-inclusive goals are included in the goals.

Note: This table was created by the author.

5

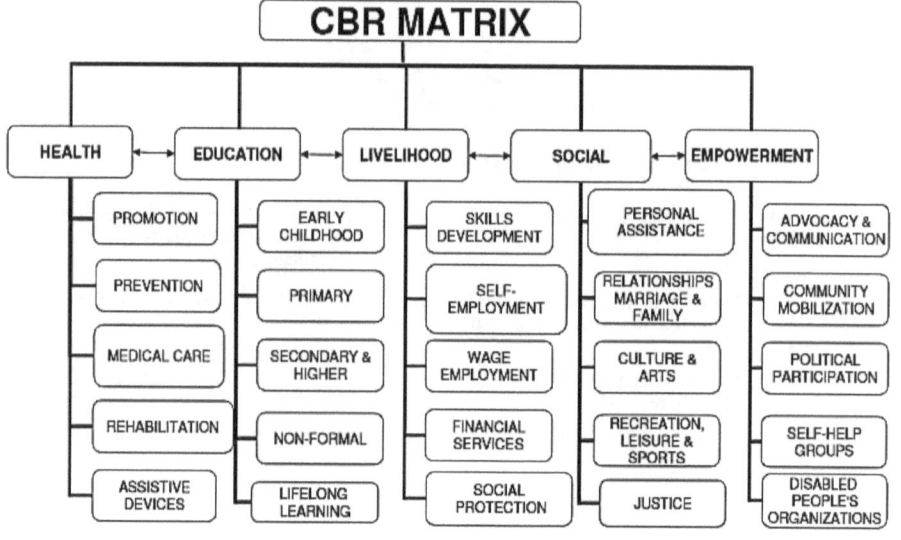

Figure 1. CBR Matrix

Note: Retrieved from the WHO et al. (2010)

The context-specific perspective in CBR

Although the potential procedure consists of these four steps, a CBR programme depends on the context. In other words, the nature of CBR appears to be bottom-up and context-specific in terms of practice. The WHO et al. (2010) emphasises the importance of sociocultural and political contexts, as follows:

> *Cultures vary, and what may be culturally appropriate for one group of people may not be the same for another group. To ensure CBR programmes are sustainable in different contexts, it is important to consider how they will affect local customs and traditions, what resistance to the programme may be expected*

and how this resistance would be managed. (p. 37)

Even though a common matrix now exists, each CBR programme will continue to demonstrate unique differences because it is influenced by a wide range of factors, e.g. physical, socioeconomic, cultural and political factors. (p. 33)

The significance of contextualisation in CBR is also reported in the literature. Cornielje et al. (2013), for instance, have demonstrated the training programme for CBR-related human resources in African contexts. CBR stakeholders should therefore consider the sociocultural, economic, and political contexts when implementing their practice and research projects. In the next section, I will discuss the concept of socioeconomic participation, which is a key term in CBR.

1.2. Basic Concept: Socioeconomic Participation of Disabled People[1]

Whilst the term and concept of 'participation' has been used as an alternative to a top-down approach in social development circles, the range of its use appears to be broad and occasionally vague (Cornwall, 2008; Cornwall & Brock, 2005; Midgley et al., 1986). After reviewing international discussions on the participation of disabled people, this section defines socioeconomic participation and discusses its multifaceted aspects using the capability approach.

---

[1] This section is an expanded version of my article (Higashida, 2018a).

7

Definition and concept

Participation is a key term in disability issues and is often used as a human rights slogan, together with 'nothing about us without us' (Cf. Werner, 1998). Indeed, the concepts of participation, inclusion, and empowerment of disabled people, have appeared in international discussions and documents, exemplified by the CRPD (UN, 2006), CBR guidelines (WHO et al., 2010), and SDGs (UN, 2015, 2018). As a result, participation has various meanings and implications. For example, the International Year of Disabled Persons held in 1981 defined 'full participation and equality' as:

> *The right of persons with disabilities to take part fully in the life and development of their societies, enjoy living conditions equal to those of other citizens, and have an equal share in improved conditions resulting from socio-economic development. (UN, 2004: no pagination)*

As Kuno (2012) has argued, this definition situates participation as both a process and a result, whilst simultaneously implicating empowerment and inclusion.

Participation of disabled people is well discussed within debates about models of disability, including medical and social models of disability (Boxes 1 and 7), although the literature suggests a need to transcend such models and form an alternative way (Beaudry, 2016). The International Classification of Impairments, Disabilities and Handicaps (ICIDH) was considered the medical model because of its focus on impairments as a cause of disabilities (WHO, 1980). The successor of the ICIDH is the International Classification of Functioning, Disability and Health (ICF) that has integrated the medical and social models of

8

disability (WHO, 2001).

As demonstrated in Figure 2, the ICF has suggested that activities and participation are influenced by their interaction with personal and environmental factors (WHO, 2001, 2013). It has also provided the perspective of 'performance', which refers to 'what a person does in their actual environment', and 'capacity', which is 'what a person does…in a standardised evaluation setting' (WHO, 2013b: p. 37). The ICF lists nine domains in activities and participation that can be either restricted or promoted by environmental and personal factors (Schneidert et al., 2003; WHO, 2001, 2013). These nine domains are: learning and applying knowledge; general tasks and demands; communication; mobility; self-care; domestic life; interpersonal interactions and relationships; major life areas; and community, social, and civic life (WHO, 2001: p.14).

Box 1: Medical Model vs. Social Model

Medical Model	Social Model
To focus on individual's impairments	To focus on social and environmental barriers
To change a person with disabilities through therapy and rehabilitation	To change society through actions and movement
To make decisions by medical and co-medical professionals	To make decisions by disabled people
To tend to use the term 'a patient' and/or 'a person with disabilities'	To tend to use the term 'disabled people' because they are disabled by society

Source: Created by the author.

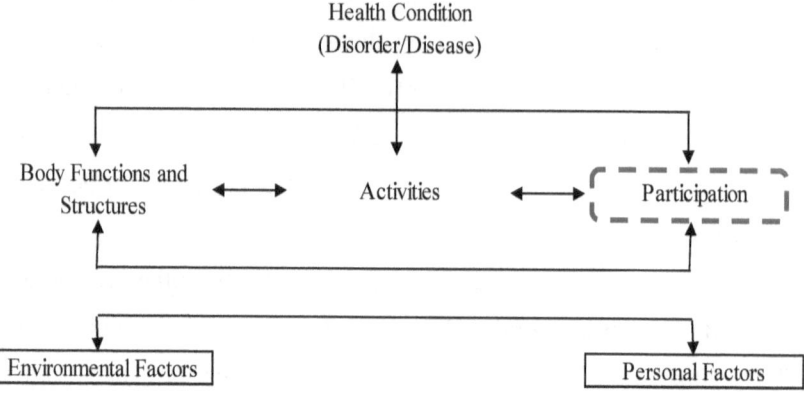

Figure 2. Interactions between the components of ICF

Note: Adapted from the WHO (2001)

With regard to 'socioeconomic' participation, I argue that the concept includes economic and non-economic aspects as researchers suggest the integration in the field of poverty and social development (Myrdal, 1970; Midgley, 1995, 2017a). Indeed, scales for the community participation of disabled people have been proposed by researchers, some of which include socioeconomic domains (e.g., Chang et al., 2013; Perenboom & Chorus, 2003; Verdonschot et al., 2009a, 2009b). These tools imply that a sole indicator is not suitable for measuring socioeconomic participation because it has multiple domains, and perhaps multiple dimensions are more appropriate.

In order to show the range of discussions about the concept in this book, this section temporarily adapts the definition of community participation by Chang et al. (2013: p.772) to broadly define the socioeconomic participation of those who are at a productive age as 'proactive involvement in activities that are intrinsically socioeconomic and occur either outside the home or as part of a non-domestic role'. The concept of socioeconomic participation will be discussed using the capability approach in the next section.

Socioeconomic participation from the perspective of the capability approach

Amartya Sen's capability approach (Sen, 1992, 1999, 2005) has been applied to many academic fields, including healthcare studies (e.g., Mitchell et al., 2017) and disability studies (Dubois & Trani, 2009; Brunner, 2015; Kuno, 2012; Mitra, 2006, 2017; Mousavi, 2015; Saleeby, 2007; Terzi, 2005; Trani et al., 2011). Given that disability is frequently discussed within one or more models of disability, such as the moral/religious (tragedy/charity model: See Box 7), the medical model, the social model (Box 1), and the ICF (e.g., Dubois & Trani, 2009; Knapp & Midgley, 2010; Kuno, 2012; Marks, 1997; Mitra, 2006, 2017), the application of the capability approach and the human development model are offered as alternatives to these models (Mitra, 2006, 2017). The background of the capability approach is different from other models of disability because it was not introduced directly as a model of disability but rather stemmed from welfare and development economics, which involves discussions about poverty and inequalities. The interpretation of disability varies in each of the models listed above, whilst the capability approach enables the comprehensive analysis of the various factors that cause deprivations (Mitra, 2006, 2017) (Box 2).

The literature discusses the participation of disabled people by applying the capability approach. As Morris (2009) has indicated, the participation of a person is considered functionings (in particular, 'doings'), whereas potential opportunities and freedom to participate are considered capabilities. A person's experiences, such as subjective experiences regarding participation, are to be included as 'beings' of

11

functionings. In real life, these beings and doings are mixed at the individual level. In addition, it is possible to grasp influences on achieved participation (functionings) and potential opportunities for participation (capabilities) through personal, social, and environmental factors, together with a consideration of available resources and commodities (Robeyns, 2005; Sen, 1992, 1999). It is also fundamental to acknowledge the choices of a disabled person to participate or not participate in any opportunities.

The following is an example of the socioeconomic participation of disabled people to explain the above concepts with reference to Sen's (1992) example on starving (p. 111–112). Even if a young woman does not participate in any social and economic activities on a regular basis (as functionings), the key point is whether she has possible opportunities for such participation or not (as capabilities). The available resources and commodities (e.g., services, assistive devices, and income for transportation expenses) are converted into possible participation opportunities (capabilities) and achieved participation (functionings) by various factors. These factors include personal (e.g., gender, age, and impairments), social (e.g., prejudice, discrimination, and information accessibility), and environmental factors (e.g., mountainous and remote areas or urban areas). Hence, the case that a disabled person could not achieve participation due to a lack of available opportunities is entirely different from the case that she decides not to do so (as choices) because of her preference, even though she has such opportunities. In other cases, disabled people and their caregivers might give up such participation because they have self-stigmatisation and just accept the situation (adaptation).

Box 2: Key Concepts in the Capability Approach

Functionings, capabilities, resources, conversion factors, choice, agency, and human diversity are key concepts in the capability approach. **Functionings** refer to 'the various things a person may value doing and being' and 'what a person is actually able to do', and capabilities refer to 'the substantive freedom to achieve alternative functioning combinations' and 'real opportunities' (Sen, 1999: p.75). Nussbaum (2001) has proposed a list of 'central human capabilities', yet that has been widely debated, with some researchers arguing that capabilities should be determined through democratic processes amongst stakeholders (Mitra, 2006, 2017; Morris, 2009; Robeyns, 2005).

Even if a person has access to **resources** and **commodities**, such as services, goods, and information, the ability to transform them into capabilities and functionings depends on conversion factors (Kuno, 2012; Mitra, 2006, 2017; Morris, 2009; Robeyns, 2005). Robeyns (2005) has clarified three main **conversion factors**: personal conversion factors (e.g., psychological and physical characteristics), social conversion factors (e.g., policies and sociocultural norms), and environmental conversion factors (e.g., geographical features). Impairments can be placed within personal characteristics (Burchardt, 2004; Mitra, 2006), although the human development model places it in health deprivations (Mitra, 2017).

In addition, a person's **choices** and **values** are fundamental to achieving the functionings that lead to his or her well-being (Sen, 1992, 1999), reflecting **human diversity** and **freedom** to achieve functionings. Choices are influenced by multiple conversion factors, including the person's preferences. Choices may be the result of adapting to a disadvantaged environment, including extreme poverty, indicating that understanding capabilities is also essential (Sen, 1992, 1999). Even if resources and commodities are available to a person, both the capability set and choices based on his or her values would be converted by personal, social, and environmental factors (Robeyns, 2005).

The concept of **agency** is also crucial to the capability approach, which has various implications for disability issues (Mitra, 2017). A person with agency is described 'as someone who acts and brings about change, and whose achievements can be judged in terms of her own values and objectives' (Sen, 1999: p.19). A person's agency achievement is described as 'the realization of goals and values she has reasons to pursue, whether or not they are connected with her own well-being' (Sen, 1992: p.56). It is thus possible to consider a distinction between well-being and choices: someone might take actions for others regardless of her own well-being in the narrow sense. Further, agency is not limited to the individual level but can be expanded to collective agency, which is defined as 'a group of individuals acting as agents not only to improve their own living conditions but also to bring about changes in their societies' (Pelenc et al., 2013: p.88).

Source: Higashida (2018a)

Like capabilities, the contents and levels of socioeconomic participation also depend on various factors, particularly the sociocultural context. Opportunities for achievable participation are likely influenced by personal, social, and environmental factors as well as resources and commodities. As Trani et al. (2011) have indicated, it is therefore essential for stakeholders to collect information on the values (i.e., what opportunities for participation should be included, and what social barriers to participation should be addressed) expressed by disabled people and community members through dialogue.

In this book, I analyse socioeconomic participation by drawing on the capability approach, but without forcefully integrating it with the ICF. There are debates about whether the capability approach complements the ICF (Saleeby et al, 2007; Morris, 2009) or whether it should distinguish itself from the ICF entirely (Mitra, 2014). The ICF uses terms similar to the capability approach, such as capacity and functioning, but the meanings are different. For instance, the meaning of functioning in the ICF is human experience related to the interaction among factors, namely body functions and structures, activities, participation, personal factors, environmental factors, and health status. The meaning and implications of functionings in the capability approach are broader than those of the ICF (Mitra, 2006). In addition, the capability approach acknowledges human diversity, freedom to achieve, and agency, thereby considering multiple conversion factors and capabilities that the ICF does not include (Morris, 2009; Mitra, 2014, 2017). Indeed, the 'ICF conceptualises functioning and disability in the context of health, and therefore does not cover circumstances that are brought about solely by socioeconomic or cultural factors' (WHO, 2013b). With regard to participation, the ICF lists cover broad domains of activities and participation, but the distinction between them is unclear and discussions on social participation seem to be inadequate (Eyssen et al., 2011). Hence,

15

this book uses the capability approach to discuss socioeconomic participation.

1.3 Practical Perspective: Developmental Social Work in CBR[2]

Whilst revealing that practical frameworks of social work in CBR are underdeveloped, this section develops the practical framework of developmental social work in CBR for promoting the socioeconomic participation of disabled people with reference to the capability approach.

Social work in CBR

Due to the bottom-up nature of CBR, practices by local stakeholders to realise the rights of disabled people, based on the CRPD, are significant. CBR emphasises a bottom-up approach for community mobilisation and capacity development of non-professionals, whilst also highlighting the empowerment of disabled people. Despite lacking professional qualifications, there are, in fact, many social workers and frontline workers who engage with social and developmental issues in developing countries (Akimoto, 2017).

Historically, the primary caregivers for disabled people at the community level are assumed to be local community members and non-professionals, such as family members, volunteers, schoolteachers, and disabled people themselves (Brinkmann, 2004; Helander et al., 1989; Peat, 1997); perhaps this perspective still applies in many fields in developing countries. The current CBR guidelines mention the target stakeholders, which include social workers, primary health workers,

---

[2] This section is based on Higashida (2017a, 2018a).

teachers, and other community development workers (WHO et al., 2010). With various types of profession, including health, education and community development, the perspective most emphasised regarding CBR would be interdisciplinary and 'skill-mix' (MacLachlan et al., 2011; Mannan et al., 2013), rather than specific professional skills and 'professional as expert' (Peat, 1997).

Research and practice emphasises the importance of social work in CBR. Lightfoot (2004) introduces CBR as an important social work strategy in disability issues, arguing that social workers can contribute to CBR because of the similar community-based approach that emphasises community organisation, coordination, and advocacy. Nagar (2015) also suggests that social workers could be important contributors to CBR. The paper presents a list of the purposes, principles, and skills of social workers, based on his work experiences in India, albeit without an academic style. Persson (2017), whilst arguing that social workers should be involved in community level activities, presents the implications of CBR in Uganda for social workers, most of whom are employed in urban governmental sectors.

However, practical frameworks of social work practices, particularly in disability issues and CBR, appear to be underdeveloped in the global South (Lightfoot, 2004; Mousavi, 2015; Van Breda, 2015; Persson, 2017). Although some papers, such as CBR guidelines (WHO et al., 2010), suggest domains and examples of practices for programme managers, process and skills of social work practices in CBR in accordance to disabled person's needs and situations are unclear. In other words, I have observed the lack of discussions in social work practices in CBR, including the active interaction between disabled people and social workers, based on theoretical frameworks and evidence. In addition, the simultaneous presence of medical and social perspectives in CBR creates a somewhat controversial situation[3]; it is therefore significant to discuss social work frameworks that shed light on socioeconomic aspects in order to prescribe the developmental practice of CBR (Veal et al, 2016). Hence, a practical framework that applies to the promotion of socioeconomic participation at the community level should be developed (Midgley & Conley, 2010). The next section will suggest that the developmental social work with the capability approach provides practical perspectives in CBR.

Developmental social work with the capability approach

Developmental social work (Box 3) is a holistic and pragmatic social work approach based on the principles of human rights and social justice that addresses poverty and socioeconomic inequalities at the individual, household, community and policy levels (Elliott & Mayadas 2001; Knapp & Midgley, 2010; Midgley, 2010). Leading scholar James Midgley, as well as researchers and professionals from the global South, such as Africa, have developed its practical approaches (e.g., Gray, 2006; Patel, 2005; Patel & Hochfeld, 2013; Van Breda, 2015). Developmental social work utilises multiple approaches and skills, in particular social investment, community-building, capacity development, and the integration of micro-macro practice (Midgley, 2010; Van Breda, 2015). Social investment is the distinctive approach in developmental social work and is defined as 'allocations to social programmes that produce returns and promote future social well-being' (Midgley, 2017: p.14). Social investment includes the aim to 'mobilize human and social capital,

---

[3] As 'concern with the use of the term "rehabilitation"' was expressed in the International Consultation to Review Community-Based Rehabilitation (WHO, 2003), it remains controversial whether 'rehabilitation' with a medical perspective is prioritised in CBR. Nevertheless, the WHO and other international actors have placed CBR in the general community and social development sphere as a strategy to address disability-related inequalities and poverty, and to promote the empowerment and inclusion of disabled people (See Section 1.1.).

facilitate employment and self-employment, promote asset accumulation, and in other ways bring about significant improvements in the material welfare of individuals, families, and communities' (Midgley, 2010: p.15).

The integration of developmental social work with disability issues has been examined by researchers, albeit in a small body of literature. Developmental social work addresses poverty and inequalities that disabled people face, whilst promoting socioeconomic participation, developing leadership for disabled people, and realising inclusion and empowerment (Knapp & Midgley, 2010). The practical framework of developmental social work, however, appears to be underdeveloped (Van Breda, 2015). Promoting socioeconomic participation, for example, is one possible entry point, but its systematic and practical frameworks need to be further developed. I suggest that the application of the capability approach to developmental social work provides practical perspectives to address poverty and socioeconomic inequalities (Box 4)

Through its micro, meso, and macro practice, developmental social work could address the deprivations of capabilities and functionings that disabled people face in their life. In other words, developmental social work responds to 'the constraints that the environment adds to a person's impairment in order to expand their capability set and to allow them to live a life which they value' (Dubois & Trani, 2009: p. 192). Beyond development, developmental social work would have the process of expanding the freedom of disabled people (Sen, 1999; Mitra, 2017). The application of the capability approach suggests that social work includes practices to develop resources and improve social structures and physical environments (Saleeby, 2007; Mitra, 2017). Developmental social work could also include direct care to improve a person's central human capabilities (Mousavi, 2015; Nussbaum, 2001; Van Breda, 2015), yet careful consideration is necessary because it might encourage mere individual interventions based on the medical model of disability (Kuno,

19

2012). Thus, it is worth clarifying that poverty and the socioeconomic inequalities facing disabled people are addressed by expanding the actual opportunities for them in developmental social work practices.[4]

Box 3: Background and Definition of Developmental Social Work

Developmental social work has emerged in international and local settings simultaneously, having its roots in traditional social work, development theories, and developmental practices in the global South (Midgley, 1995, 2010, 2013; Patel & Hochfeld, 2013). Research and practice since the 1970s, including that of social workers and the International Consortium for Social Development (formerly the Inter-University Consortium for International Development), has developed the perspective and concept of social development and developmental social work (Midgley, 1978, 1995, 2010). In particular, researchers and practitioners of social work in Africa have contributed significantly to innovation in and development of the theory and practice. One of the contexts from

---

[4] The concepts of choices and agency also have implications for developmental social work. Developmental social workers respect self-determination by disabled people, whilst supporting their decision-making if necessary. In some cases, reflection on the social workers' practice and relationship with disabled people, including potential paternalistic interventions, is required. In addition, the concept of agency emphasises the importance of human rights as well as the importance of choices for disabled people. Disabled people promote their human rights and empowerment through political participation, advocacy, and collective movement, and their claims may include criticism of professionals, including in the social work practice (Knapp & Midgley, 2010; Oliver & Barnes, 1998). This might pose a difficult dilemma for social workers between prioritising a person's agency or their well-being. There is no one-size-fits-all answer to this issue, but developmental social workers can find reasonable practice with disabled people and other stakeholders through substantial dialogue.

20

which developmental social work emerged, particularly in South Africa, was the White Paper for Social Welfare in 1997; this is because the national government policy applied the developmental approach to social work and welfare after the end of apartheid (Midgley, 1995, 2010; Patel & Hochfeld, 2013).

Due to the complicated history and multiple factors that have influenced the development of the theory and practice, developmental social work does not appear to have a consistent definition. Rather, the range of discussion is quite broad (Lombard, 2008; Midgley, 2010, 2013; Patel & Hochfeld, 2013). Nonetheless, Patel attempts to define developmental social work as follows: 'practical and appropriate application of social development knowledge, skills and values to social work processes to enhance the well-being of individuals, families, households, groups, organizations and communities in their social context' (Patel, 2005: pp.206–207). An implication of this definition is the integrated macro- and micro-dimensions.

Furthermore, in Patel's definition of developmental social work, social development is a key concept because of its application to social work. Influenced by social development theories, such as the capability approach, Midgley (2013) suggests the definition of social development as 'a process of planned social change designed to promote the well-being of the population as a whole within the context of a dynamic multifaceted development process' (p.13).

Source: Higashida (2017a)

Box 4: Capability Approach in Social Work

The application of the capability approach to social work and social welfare, including developmental social work, has been examined by several researchers (Braber, 2013; Saleeby, 2007; Veal et al., 2016). For example, Midgley (2017) has argued 'the need for new policies and programmes that invest in human capabilities rather than transferring resources to passive welfare recipients' (p.17), whilst also referring to Sen's capability approach in his other papers on developmental social work (e.g., Midgley, 2010). However, the relationship between developmental social work and the capability approach does not appear to have been discussed in detail in the literature. Possible reasons for this absence are that each has a different focus, even though both developmental social work and the capability approach address poverty and inequalities. Developmental social work tends to focus on the improvement of material well-being for persons and communities (Midgley, 2010), whereas the capability approach tends to focus on potential opportunities and achieved functionings that lead to the well-being of a person (Robeyns, 2005). With respect to its nature, developmental social work emphasises practice, whereas the capability approach emphasises analysis. I argue that the application of the capability approach to developmental social work in disability issues is both possible and helpful for understanding the socioeconomic participation of disabled people.

Source: Higashida (2018a)

Developmental social work for promoting socioeconomic participation

This section proposes the practical framework of developmental social work in disability issues and CBR applying the capability approach. The ultimate values of developmental social work in CBR involve human rights, social justice, and socioeconomic equality (Elliott & Mayadas, 2001). The targets of developmental social work practice emphasise the importance of promoting the socioeconomic participation of disabled people, although it is not limited to participation in specific domains (Midgley, 2010, 2017a). Developmental social work tackles the constraints faced by disabled people because of multiple factors in society, in order to expand their actual opportunities and allow them to choose the ones they value (Dubois & Trani, 2009; Mitra, 2006, 2017; Saleeby, 2007).

In line with this framework of developmental social work in disability issues, its practice expands socioeconomic participation opportunities through engagements with health deprivations, resource shortages, and structural barriers in society, all whilst considering human diversities (Mitra, 2017). Developmental social work therefore covers a range from practice in the community to social change and policy-making (Elliott & Mayadas, 2001; Midgley, 2010). Since one of the distinctive approaches of developmental social work is social investment, which addresses poverty and socioeconomic inequalities (Midgley, 2010, 2017a), it is the preferred practice to expand actual opportunities for disabled people to enjoy socioeconomic participation.

Referring to the literature (Knapp & Midgley, 2010; Midgley, 2010; Saleeby, 2007; Van Breda, 2015), I summarise dimensions of developmental social work for the promotion of socioeconomic participation based on the application of the capability approach (Kuno,

23

2012; Morris, 2009; Robeyns, 2005; Sen, 1992, 1999). Figure 3 illustrates the conceptual framework that integrates the micro, meso, and macro practices of developmental social work. Five squares in the figure indicate key components of the capability approach: resources, conversion factors, capability set (freedom to participate), choice, and achieved functionings (participation). The black arrows represent potential interactions between these components, whereas grey arrows indicate the entry points of developmental social work practice in CBR. Grey arrows also imply the bidirectional relationships: the influence of developmental social work practice on each component and the feedback of each component on developmental social work practice. Although Van Breda (2015) has described six stages of developmental social casework at the individual level (engagement, assessment, planning, implementation, evaluation, and termination), the order of the process that I proposed is non-linear so as to respond to the personal and local context and micro-macro dynamic practices.

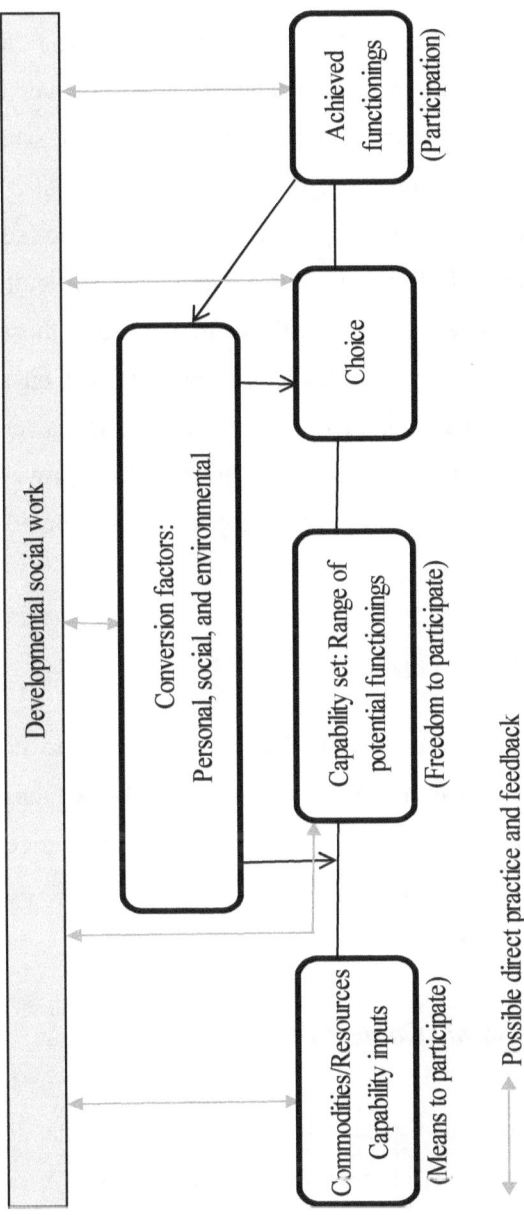

Figure 3. Conceptual framework of the capability approach applied to developmental social work for promoting a person's participation

Note: Adapted from Higashida (2018a), making with reference to Robeyns (2005) and Trani et al. (2011).

25

I argue that the role of developmental social work includes establishing available resources and changing conversion factors in society in order to enhance a person's capability set, whilst identifying his or her needs and deprived capabilities. I also suggest that developmental social work practices could provide support for the decision-making of disabled people who have difficulties and could coordinate available resources with them. That said, those who conduct developmental social work practices need to reflect on some potential issues in social casework such as paternalism and power relationships. Thus, this framework provides useful guidance to improve the well-being and enhance the agency of disabled people (See Section 10.1).

1.4. Sri Lankan Context

Drawing on these frameworks, it is important to consider related policy and systems in a specific context. This book focuses on CBR in Sri Lanka where I found a need for both action and research. In the dawning age of global CBR in the 1980s, a CBR programme was initiated in Sri Lanka.

Socioeconomic Context in Sri Lanka

The Democratic Socialist Republic of Sri Lanka, formerly called 'Ceylon', is located in South Asia. Sri Lanka is a multi-ethnic, multi-religious, and multi-lingual country. The socioeconomic features in the country are significant contexts for examining the socioeconomic participation of individuals. As summarised in Table 2, this section analysed the socioeconomic indicators and related data using reports of international organisations (IMF, 2018; UNDP, 2018; UNESCO, 2018) and the government (Department of Census and Statistics [DCS], 2017, 2018). Some of the indicators show that Sri Lanka has promoted socioeconomic and human development.

According to International Monetary Fund (IMF, 2018), economic conditions in Sri Lanka improved after the end of a 26-year civil war in 2009, exemplified by the high economic growth rate at 9.1% in 2012. Although the percent rate of the increase in gross domestic products (GDP) decreased between 2014 and 2017, the rate remained between 3.1% and 5.0% (IMF, 2018). GDP per capita also increased by approximately two times from USD 2,057 in 2009 to USD 4,073 in 2018 (CEIC, 2018). The poverty rate, which is calculated by the comparison of the monthly real per capita expenditure with the official poverty lines, decreased from 15.2% in 2006 to 6.7% in 2012/2013 and 4.1% in 2016 (DCS, 2017).[5]

---

[5] The current economic and political relationship between China and Sri Lanka has been complex (Lim & Mukherjee, 2017). Since the country's election in 2015, related issues, including Sri Lanka's indebtedness to China, have been debated. Although this paper will not discuss the detail because it is not the main topic, it is required for considering the influence of such external power on the socioeconomic situation in Sri Lanka.

Table 2 The indicators in socioeconomic and human development dimensions in Sri Lanka

Subject Descriptor	Units	1990/9	2000	2009	2010	2011	2012	2013	2014	2015	2016	2017
Gross domestic product, constant prices	Percent change	6.2	8.4	3.5	8.0	8.4	9.1	3.4	5.0	5.0	4.5	3.1
Human Development Index[2]	Index	0.63	0.69	N/A	0.75	0.75	0.76	0.76	0.76	0.77	0.77	0.77
Life expectancy at birth[2]	Years	69.5	71.0	74.3	74.4	74.5	74.6	74.7	74.9	75.1	75.3	75.5
Employment to population ratio[2]	% ages 15 and older	51.2*	52.5	N/A	52.0	52.1	51.4	52.6	51.7	51.4	51.4	51.4
Employment in agriculture[2]	% of total employment	42.8*	41.3	32.5[4]	33.6	33.1	31.0	29.8	28.5	28.1	27.5	26.7
Employment in services[2]	% of total employment	30.6*	35.4	42.4[4]	41.5	42.8	42.9	44.1	45.1	46.4	47.0	47.7
Labour force participation rate[2]	% ages 15 and older	62.5*	56.9	54.1[4]	54.7	54.4	53.5	55.0	54.1	53.9	53.8	53.5
Unemployment, total[2]	% of labour force	14.7*	7.7	5.9[4]	4.9	4.1	3.9	4.4	4.4	4.7	4.4	4.1
Working poor at PPP$3.10 a day[2]	% of total employment	38.3*	30.6	N/A	13.8	13.1	12.1	12.2	11.6	11.1	10.7	10.1
Net enrolment rate, primary education[3]	%	N/A	N/A	93.3	94.9	95.1	95.4	96.4	97.2	98.9	98.9	99.1
Expected years of schooling[2]	Years	11.3	12.5	13.5	13.6	13.7	13.8	13.8	13.9	13.9	13.9	13.9

Note: This table was created by the author. * indicates the date in 1991. Source: 1) IMF (2018), 2) UNDP (2018), 3) UNESCO (2018), 4) DCS (2018)

United Nations Development Programme (UNDP, 2018) demonstrates that the value of the human development index (HDI), which is used to measure a country's achievement in socioeconomic dimensions, is 0.770 in Sri Lanka. The rank of Sri Lanka is 76 out of 189 countries in 2017, and its HDI value is classified under the high human development category. The HDI value in Sri Lanka is higher than average in South Asia at 0.638 as well as that in India at 0.640 and that in Pakistan at 0.562. Indeed, the life expectancy at birth in Sri Lanka is at 75.5 years which are higher than the average of the South Asia region at 69.3 years, whilst mean years of schooling in Sri Lanka is at 10.9 years which are also higher than the average in the region at 6.4. In addition, GNI per capita is USD 11,326 that is higher than the average in South Asia at USD 6,473.

In terms of education, the expected years of schooling have been longer than 13 years in Sri Lanka since 2010, which are higher than average in South Asia at 11.9 years (UNDP, 2018; UNESCO, 2018). The net enrolment rate in primary education reached 99% in 2017, tending a slight difference between males and females (UNESCO, 2018). Population with at least some secondary education aged 25 years and older are 82.8%, with males at 83.1% and females at 82.6%, which is larger than the average in South Asia (males at 60.6% and females at 39.8%) (UNDP, 2018). Furthermore, the primary school dropout rate is 1.6% in 2017 (UNDP, 2018).

Regarding work and employment, Department of Census and Statistics (DCS, 2018) shows that the labour force participation rate, which illustrates percentage of a country's working-age population, has been between 53.5% and 55.0% from 2009 to 2017 in Sri Lanka. 'Economically inactive population', including full-time students, retired persons, and disabled people ('Infirmed/Disabled'), is 45.9% in 2017.

The highest rate of the reported reasons is 'engaged in housework' at 46.3%, having a gender difference with females at 60.5% and males at 4.9%. The rate is followed by 'engaged in studies' at 21.6% and 'Retired/Old age' at 20.3%. The fourth highest rate is 'Physically illness/Disabled' at 8.0%, with males at 15.9% and females at 5.3%. Amongst the 'economically inactive population', the highest rate group of the level of education is Grade 6 – 10 at 44.8%, followed by General Certificate of Education, Ordinary Level (G.C.E., O/L) at 23.0% and Grade 5 and below at 19.2% (DCS, 2018).

The employment to population ratio amongst those aged 15 years and older has been between 51.4% and 52.5% since 2010 (UNDP, 2018). The employment rate is 95.8% with males at 97.1% and females at 93.5% in 2017, having no significant difference between urban areas at 95.6% and rural areas at 95.9% (DCS, 2018). The share of employment in agriculture decreased from 40% in 2000 to 26.7 in 2017, whereas that of employment in services increased from 35.4% in 2000 to 47.7% in 2017 (DCS, 2018).

The unemployment rate has been between 3.9% and 4.9% since 2010 (UNDP, 2018). The rate is 4.2% in 2017 with males at 2.9% and females at 6.5%, having a slight difference between urban areas at 4.4% and rural areas at 4.1% (DCS, 2018). The percentage of youth who are not in school or employment was 27.7% in 2014.

Overview of Sri Lankan disability issues and CBR

This section gives an overview of the basic aspects of disability issues and the national CBR programme in Sri Lanka. I clarify the reasons for selecting it as a case study country, arguing that it would be a good example for analysing the practices from the developmental social work perspective. I also touch upon challenges facing the national CBR programme (See also Chapter 2).

According to the census (DCS, 2012), approximately 8.7% of the population experience some type of functional difficulty, including vision loss (61.6%), difficulty walking (45.4%), hearing loss (24.0%), reduced cognition (21.2%), self-care (12.2%), and/or communication issues (11.2%). Officially 111,079 disabled people were recorded on the CBR unit's database as of August 2017 (December 2017 field notes).

In addition to these disability statistics, it is also important to understand the sociocultural and religious aspects of disabilities in Sri Lanka. Common Sinhalese words include 'Aabaadhita' (ආබාධිත), which means 'disabled' and 'Aabaadhitayaa' (ආබාධිතයා), which means 'the disabled', distinguishing them from 'normal' people and focusing on lack of ability (Liyanage, 2017). For this reason, some stakeholders, including the government sector, use alternative expressions, such as: 'Wisheesa awashyataa ati aya', meaning 'a person with special needs', and 'Aabaadha sahita pudgalaya' (ආබාධ සහිත පුද්ගලයා), meaning 'people with disabilities'. In addition, there is complexity of public attitudes towards disability, exemplified by disabled veterans who are treated differently from others. Nevertheless, a negative social image of disability has been common in Sri Lanka's customs (Liyanage, 2017). Indeed, the literature reveals that disabled people have restricted opportunities to participate in social activities, confirming the relationship between poverty and disability (Kumara & Gunewardena, 2017; Murthy et al., 2018).[6]

In such a sociocultural context, the Sri Lankan government has implemented policies to tackle the limited socioeconomic participation of disabled people, in cooperation with NGOs. Policies and practices range from efforts to empower disabled people to inclusive approaches for all

---

[6] This paragraph is based on Higashida (2019a).

people, including disabled people (Mendis, 2003). As demonstrated in Table 3, the government of Sri Lanka has officially implemented CBR projects and programmes since the early 1980s, when CBR emerged as a global strategy (Kumara, 2016; Ministry of Social Services [MSS], 2012a; Ministry of Social Services and Social Welfare, 2008). The purpose of the Sri Lanka's CBR programme is defined as: 'empowering disabled persons with knowledge and skills to enable them to enjoy their rights and perform their duties and responsibilities in national development within the prevailing socioeconomic system and creating opportunities through the ongoing social development programmes' (Ministry of Social Empowerment and Welfare, 2016: p. 22).[7] The programme has been implemented within 331 Divisional Secretariats (DSs) in 25 districts, which cover all of the administrative divisions in Sri Lanka. Non-governmental organisations (NGOs) also implement CBR programme in collaboration with the Ministry of Social Services (MSS) and renamed ministries[8].

With regard to social services and CBR, the MSS might face various issues related to marginalisation amongst multisectors. At the national level, the CBR programme appeared to be given lower priority amongst the social development programmes. The national CBR programme in the MSS was downgraded to the department level at the end of 2014. The MSS (2012a) also mentions the constraints on the programme: poor planning, not following the sequence of stages when expanding the programme, inadequate or lack of multisectoral collaboration, and inadequacies in capacity building (See also Chapter 2).

---

[7] The objective of the Sri Lankan national CBR programme in 2013 was '(re)ehabilitation of persons with disabilities to enable them to enjoy their rights and perform responsibilities and create opportunities through social development programmes to integrate them into the society' (MSS, 2013, p.24).

[8] The name and structure of the ministry has changed frequently. The current name as of March 2019 is the Ministry of Primary Industries and Social Empowerment. This study uses tentative terms, such as the ministry (and department) responsible for social services (See Chapter 2).

Table 3: History of CBR and disability laws in Sri Lanka

Year	Legislation/Policy	Notes	National Level Events
16C–17C		Traditional medicine, including Ayurveda and horoscopes, was already in use.[1]	
1863	Ceylon Lunacy Ordinance	Compulsory segregation policy[2]	Colonised by Britain (1796–1948)
1912	First education programme for disabled children[3]	Established by a British Christian association	
1948			Independence proclaimed as 'Ceylon'
1956	Mental Disease Act		
1958			Sinhala Only Act
1966	Major revision of Mental Health Ordinance	Shift from hospitalisation to community-based psychiatry and rehabilitation[4]	
1968	Establishment of psychiatric training	University of Colombo[5]	
1972			Renamed 'Sri Lanka'. Changed to 'Democratic Socialist Republic of Sri Lanka' in 1978.
1979	Introduction of community-based rehabilitation (CBR) into Sri Lanka	Some undocumented attempts by actors, including Dr Padmani Mendis	
1981	The prototype CBR manual was tested in villages in Sri Lanka.	The manual was partly translated into Sinhalese.[6]	
1982	WHO interregional consultation for CBR held in Colombo.	The meeting was inaugurated by the Ministry of Health.[6]	

	Survey of child mental health problems within the primary health care system	
1983		Start of the civil war
1984	Pilot project focusing on teacher training	Sponsored by UNICEF since 1984
1988	Public Administration Circular No. 27/88	To allocate 3% of job opportunities in the public sector to disabled people
1993	Ratification of the Asian and Pacific Decade Declaration	
1994	National CBR programme[7]	Approved as a national programme in 1992 and handed over to the ministry responsible for Social Services in 1994
1996	Protection of the Rights of Persons with Disabilities Act No. 28 of 1996	The National Council for Coordinating the Work of Disability Organizations submitted the proposal in 1994. [8]
	Social Security Board Act, No. 17 of 1996	Benefit scheme for self-employed people
1999	Social Security Board (Amendment) Act, No. 33 of 1999;	
	Ranaviru Seva Act, No. 54 of 1999	For the care and rehabilitation of the armed forces and police
2003	National Policy on Disability[9]	
	Protection of the Rights of Persons with Disabilities (Amendment) Act, No. 33 of 2003	
2004		Indian Ocean earthquake and tsunami
2005	Mental Health Policy	Policy from 2005 to 2015[10]

2007	Federation of Visually Handicapped Act	
2009		End of the civil war
2011	National Action Plan for the Protection and Promotion of Human Rights 2011–2016	'Inadequate community-based rehabilitation programmes'
2012	Draft of CBR five-year action plan[11]	Not implemented
2013	National action plan for disability	Drafted by the Ministry of Social Services and the Ministry of Health
2015	100 day programme[12]	Due to the regime change
2016	Ratification of the Convention on the Rights of Persons with Disabilities (CRPD)	Signed in March 2007

Note: Adapted from Higashida (2018b) using the following sources: 1) Kuruppuarachchi & Rajakaruna (1999); 2) Kato (2009); 3) Campbell (2011); 4) WHO (2011); 5) Ranasinghe et al. (2011); 6) WHO (1982); 7) FIT (2002); 8) Mendis (1997); 9) Ministry of Social Welfare (2003); 10) Mental Health Directorate (2005); 11) Ministry of Social Services (2012a); 12) Minister of Social Services, Welfare and Livestock Development (2015)

The reasons for selecting Sri Lanka as a case country

Sri Lanka was selected as a case country for the following reasons. First, the government has implemented a national CBR programme with community-based activities for a long period of time. It is therefore a suitable case for exploring the grassroots-level practice by local workers under the national-level policy. This is also consistent with the developmental perspective that emphasises the importance of not only community-level practices but also the government commitment (Midgley & Conley, 2010). Indeed, the WHO (2013a) selected Sri Lanka as one of its regional case studies in the Southeast Asian region, where several governments were implementing the community-level practices (See also Chapter 2).

Second, Sri Lankan CBR is a good case for analysing the practices by local workers, whose practices can be analysed from the developmental social work perspective. In terms of the public sector, social services officer (SSOs)—and some other officers, such as social development assistants, and development officers who are local government officers attached to the DSs, are mainly in charge of the CBR programme at the grassroots level (MSS, 2013). The SSOs are expected to conduct inclusive programmes by collaboration with other governmental sectors and to coordinate CBR volunteers who support disabled people at the grassroots level.

Third, Sri Lanka's domestic circumstances, where a 26-year civil war only ended in 2009, provide a valuable context for examining the CBR's impact on various issues that are unlikely to be managed well (Peiris-John et al., 2014; See also Chapter 5).

1.5. Research Gaps

Research gaps in Sri Lankan CBR

When it comes to research focusing on CBR in developing countries, its impacts on disabled people's participation appear to be under-represented in the literature. For instance, Finkenflügel et al. (2005) found that there were only five articles on participation, one descriptive study and four theoretical papers. Additional review of the literature was conducted using on-line database searches for English articles from 2006 onwards (PubMed, Scopus, and Web of Science: accessed 15 April 2017). Six articles with titles that include 'participation' and 'community-based rehabilitation' (and/or 'CBR') have been identified using these electronic databases. Only four papers, including one article from an emerging country (India), discuss CBR and participation. Biggeri et al. (2014) have revealed the significant and positive impact of interventions, such as participation in CBR, on the quality of life of participants in India. However, the amount of evidence-based research and practice, including studies on the association between the related practices and the participation of disabled people, remains limited in developing countries.

The practice and effectiveness of CBR and the socioeconomic status of disabled people in Sri Lanka has rarely been studied or presented. According to a review (Peiris-John et al., 2014), impacts and issues of CBR and related practices in Sri Lanka are under-documented in the literature. Some international organisations report on education (UNICEF, 2003) and employment opportunities (World Bank, 2014) in relation to disability issues. Moreover, Murthy et al. (2018) recently attempted to describe the situation of activity limitation and social participation of disabled people in Sri Lanka, whilst focusing mainly on the association with the level of functional difficulties and disabilities. Nonetheless, there is a gap between policy, practice, and research, as Peiris-John et al. (2014) state that '[n]one of the studies eligible for review evaluated the provision of support services or training needed by people with disability' (p.3).

Research gaps in Sri Lankan Social Work

There is also a research gap of social work in the context of Sri Lanka. The Sri Lanka School of Social Work is run administratively under the National Institute of Social Development (NISD) and offers Diploma, Bachelor's, and Master's degree courses in social work. These courses are described as education based on western-rooted professional social work (Herath & Wickramasinghe, 2015). The NISD also explores indigenous social work education that incorporates the faith-based social work approach (Subramaniam, Hatta, & Vasudevan, 2014). In addition to formal education, social work activities are conducted at the grassroots level by Buddhist monks (Herath & Wickramasinghe, 2015), local government officers such as SSOs in the government sector, and NGO staff. However, researchers point out that the educational system is not closely related to the provision of professional human resources for the government sector (Attanayake, 2016; NISD, 2017; Subramaniam, Hatta, & Vasudevan, 2014: See also Chapter 2). The comprehensive situation of social work in disability issues has not been examined in the Sri Lankan context. Hence, the stakeholders' practices, including the interaction of developmental social work with disabled people, must be examined.

1.6. Overall Purpose, Structure and Caveats

This research project aims to examine the socioeconomic

38

participation of disabled people in rural Sri Lanka, with the overall purpose to explore practical strategies to promote their participation from the perspective of developmental social work. Research questions (RQs) for the field project are as follows:

RQ. 1) To what extent and how do disabled people participate in socioeconomic activities?

RQ. 2) What factors are associated with socioeconomic participation of disabled people?

RQ. 3) How do developmental social work practices in CBR promote socioeconomic participation of disabled people?

The structure of this dissertation is as follows (Figure 4). Chapter 2 is a prerequisite for field research and practices, whilst indicating the relationship with findings from Chapter 4 to Chapter 9. This examines stakeholder-influenced implementation dynamics and the gaps between CBR policy and practice in Sri Lanka, thereby revealing the challenges facing the systems. Drawing on the policy analysis triangle, I analyse four components—the actors, context, process, and content—using related documents.

Chapter 3 provides the outline of the methodology of the research project in rural Sri Lanka. It consists of methods, field contexts, my positionality, and overall process during the project. It also includes information on distinctive features of each study site; with regard to the current situation of CBR, the areas studied consist of a developing area in the Western Province, a post-conflict area in the Northern Province, and a model area of CBR in the North-central Province. In addition, context-specific research through dialogues, non-linear process, and pragmatism are stressed as essential strategic concepts at the community level.

Chapters 4 to 6 present the situation analysis on socioeconomic participation of disabled people in three districts, as well as on local resources, stakeholders, and sociocultural contexts, from the developmental social work perspective. In particular, each chapter attempts to examine the extent and process of socioeconomic participation of disabled people, whilst also revealing factors and dynamics that are associated with the opportunities for their participation.

Chapters 7 to 9 analyse developmental social work practices in the model area of CBR in the North-central Province. It explores the strategy and roles of CBR stakeholders, specifically focusing on SSOs, from the developmental social work perspective. An indigenous approach, social investment, comprehensive and multisectoral approach, and development of existing local resources are also pointed out at the community level. Moreover, it discusses sustainability and capacity building in the local community.

Chapter 10 integrates all findings comprehensively and specifies their implications for developmental social work practices in rural Sri Lanka. This final chapter summarises the key issues and discusses limitations of this research project, followed by recommendations for future research.

Like any other literature, this paper comes with the following caveats. This research project does not claim to standardise the analytic methodology in disability issues and generalise the developmental social work strategies that can be applicable in any area in Sri Lanka and other regions; rather it presents contextualised and positioned practices. Therefore, the intention of this paper is to provide practical ideas and findings that could be further extended in future research and practice.

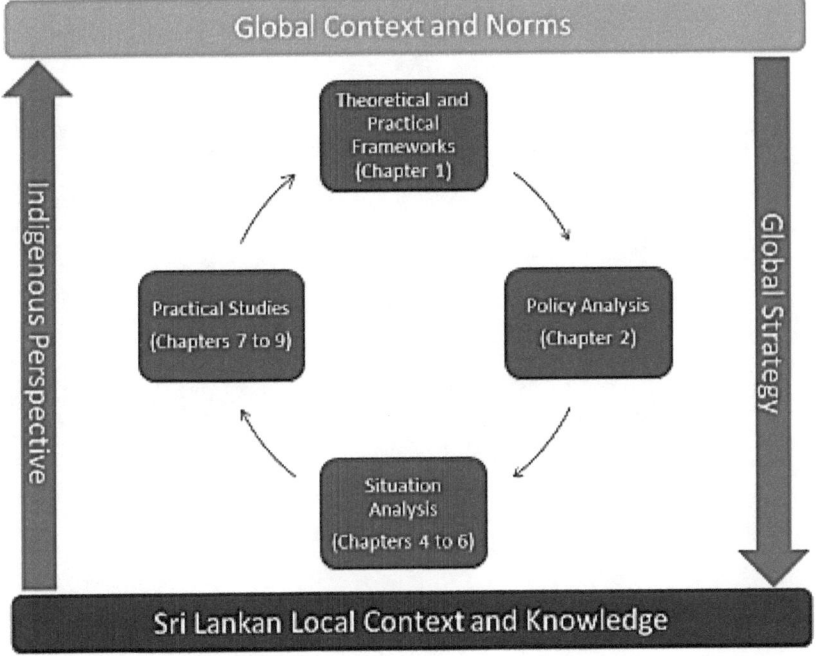

Figure 4. Structure of this book

Note: This figure was created by the author.

CHAPTER TWO

Sri Lankan CBR Policy And Practice

Given that social exclusion is a key issue for disabled people in South Asia, the promotion of their empowerment and inclusion will require the strengthening of systems of CBID through the policy and practice of CBR (Klasing, 2007; WHO, 2013a). A strategic approach to CBR, related policies based on the needs of disabled people, and evidence of feasibility and cost-effectiveness are ideally used to strengthen disability-inclusive systems, in collaboration with various stakeholders (Balabanova et al., 2011; Buse et al., 2012; Campbell & Ikegami, 1998). Studies of the relationship between CBR policies and practices suggest that strengthening these systems will have a significant impact (Kuipers & Hartley, 2006; Kuipers et al., 2008; Hartley & Okune, 2008) as implementation gaps between planned policies and their achieved results are a common issue (e.g. Haines, Kuruvilla & Borchert, 2004; Ridde, 2008). It is therefore important to consider the nexus between the macro level of CBR policies and the meso and micro levels of their practical implementation throughout the region.

It is crucial for stakeholders to understand how CBR is carried out in practice under Sri Lanka's planned policy, and for them to contribute their own policy perspectives in order to support a disability-inclusive society. The objective of this study is to examine stakeholder-influenced implementation dynamics and the gaps between CBR policy and developmental social work practice in Sri Lanka, with the overall purpose of revealing the challenges facing the system as it moves towards realising CBID. The study is guided by the following research questions:

How has the national CBR policy been implemented at the grassroots level in Sri Lanka?

What challenges do the actors and systems currently engaged with disability issues face?'

This study uses a policy analysis triangle with a relational approach perspective (Buse et al., 2012; Walt, 1994; Walt & Gilson, 1994). This framework has been applied to many public health studies as it is a convenient and comprehensive approach (e.g. Etiaba et al., 2015; May et al., 2014; Moshiri et al., 2016). The policy analysis triangle (Box 5) can help to explore the neglected place of politics in health-related policies, and can reveal the complex interactions between multiple factors (Buse et al., 2012).

Box 5: Policy Analysis Triangle

Theoretically and visually, the context, process, and content are positioned at each corner of the triangle, whilst the actors are located in its centre. Instead of considering each component separately, the dynamics amongst the four components are analysed, together with the variations in each component (Buse, Mays & Walt 2012).

Drawing on the triangle's framework, this study analyses the following aspects: 1) the '**actors**', who are stakeholders in the implementation of CBR policies, ranging from individuals to organisations; 2) the '**context**', which includes factors that can potentially influence policies, whether directly or indirectly, such as the sociocultural and administrative backgrounds underpinning aspects of CBR implementation; 3) the '**process**', which is the historical dynamics of policies, including time-series and events that occurred when CBR policy was being developed and implemented; and 4) the '**content**', which refers to the actual and substantial details of CBR policy implementation, including the activities of actors at the national and grassroots levels.

Source: Higashida (2018b),
making with reference to Buse et al. (2012).

2.1. Actors

This section provides an overview of the stakeholders' involvement in the implementation of the CBR programme, whilst also revealing issues related to the other three components of the policy triangle. The MSS and the renamed ministries, and the Department of Social Services, have played an important role in the implementation of the CBR programme at the national level. Disabled people, their families, DPOs, non-professional community volunteers, and frontline officers are the key actors at the district and divisional levels. Other stakeholders, such as NGOs and international organisations, have also been involved in Sri Lanka's CBR programme.

At the national level, the MSS, the renamed ministries[9], and the Department of Social Services, particularly its CBR unit, have implemented the programme, taking responsibility for budget management, planning, monitoring, and training. They have also taken responsibility for coordinating multisectoral programmes with other ministries and departments. The Ministry of Health may have relatively strong ties to the MSS (Ministry of Health, 2014) and has, for example, carried out the early identification of disabled children since the 1980s (FIT, 2002; WHO, 1982, 2012). These two ministries were previously integrated under one Minister of Health and Social Services for a short time, but the current separate system, with its vertically divided administrative structure, has weakened the relationship (WHO, 2012).

The NISD—formerly the Sri Lanka School of Social Work[10]—has been administratively placed under the ministry responsible for social

---

[9] The current name as of March 2019 is the Ministry of Primary Industries and Social Empowerment (Section 2.4).
[10] An NGO established the Institute of Social Work in 1952. It was developed as a government institute and renamed the Ceylon School of Social Work in 1964 and the Sri Lanka School of Social Work in 1972. The NISD was established in 1992 and the School of Social Work was brought under the NISD.

services. It was one of main actors in CBR before the nationalisation of the programme which was handed over to the ministry in 1994 (Herath, 2014). The NISD now offers diploma, Bachelor's, and Master's degree courses in social work. However, researchers point out that the educational system is not closely related to the provision of professional human resources for the government sector,[11] despite offering students field-training programmes at NGOs and the government sector, and courses that some frontline workers have taken (Attanayake, 2016; NISD, 2017; Subramaniam et al., 2014).

At the divisional level, a CBR core group[12] that includes SSOs and other frontline officers is responsible for CBR activities, in cooperation with local stakeholders (Kumara, 2016; WHO, 2013a). As of August 2014, 472 officers were assigned to CBR across the country, although they have multiple responsibilities apart from CBR (August 2014 field notes). These local government officers are expected to have knowledge and skills acquired through on-the-job and off-the-job training,[13] which is coordinated by the ministry and department responsible for social services. The SSOs, who have CBR as one of their responsibilities, are expected to conduct multisectoral activities with other sectors at the divisional level. These sectors include the Medical Officer of Health (MOH), zonal education offices and schools, the government sections in

---

[11] According to the NISD's (2017) report based on a brief survey, the employment percentage of graduates who obtained Bachelor of Social Work from the institute in 2012/2016 is 74%. Whilst 54% of them obtained a job opportunity at a local or international NGO, 22% found employment in the government sector. In terms of therapists, the School of Physiotherapy and Occupational Therapy, run by the National Hospital of Sri Lanka, implements a field-training programme at the community level (Peat 1997).

[12] According to central government officers, it is not now called 'CBR core group (officer)' due to a recent change of the CBR policy (December 2017 field notes). This study tentatively focusses on SSOs.

[13] According to the Hill Country Disabled Group (no date), 18-day training sessions were provided for these officers at some point in the 2000s. A central government officer stated that they are considering restarting the training for SSOs and other CBR stakeholders, although 21-day training sessions for the CBR core group officers had previously been implemented (December 2017 field notes).

charge of cultural and religious affairs, the Samurdhi Authority that conducts poverty reduction and development programmes, and 'Grama Niladhari' who provides first-contact public service counters for villagers (MSS, 2012a).

Disabled people and their families may theoretically be involved at any level of the programme, although not all disabled people necessarily participate in the programme. The positionality of disabled people varies, such as advocates and beneficiaries (Rifkin & Kangare, 2002). Disabled people are encouraged to participate in empowerment and collective activities, such as DPOs and self-help groups. There are various kinds of DPOs and related groups, including self-help ('Swashakthi') groups supported by SSOs in each division. With regard to the number of beneficiaries, 55.1% of the 106,900 disabled people identified by the government sector were supported through CBR as of 2007 (WHO, 2013a). However, the reliability of this figure and the nature of the impact are uncertain; Chapter 4 suggests that there may only be low-level socioeconomic participation opportunities for disabled people in rural areas.

Community volunteers and leaders are important contributors to the CBR programme, but the system of capacity development is often underdeveloped. The MSS reported in 2012 that 8,127 volunteers and 7,827 community leaders had been trained to conduct CBR activities (MSS, 2012b). Community volunteers are recruited from villages by SSOs and other frontline officers. Although it is possible for all villagers to be appointed, including elderly, young, disabled people, and their family members, it is elderly committee members who are most likely to work as volunteers (WHO, 2013a; See also Chapter 8). Given that young volunteers tend to leave their villages in search of job opportunities, the appointment of elderly volunteers may be a realistic solution (WHO, 2013a). Their supportive activities are coordinated by CBR related

47

officers, in particular SSOs. However, according to my 2014 field notes and the reports of three Japanese social workers (JSWs) in 2014–2016, the community-based activities run by CBR volunteers are largely inactive. In several divisions, the CBR volunteers have been officially registered by name, but have not been given any substantial activities.[14] This information suggests that the system may be unsustainable and inactive when it comes to capacity development.

Other stakeholders, particularly NGOs, have also been involved with CBR at the grassroots level. For example, Sarvodaya (an organisation whose mission is discussed in the following section), FRIDSRO, Navajeevana, AKASA, the Christian Children's Fund, and the Sri Lanka Spinal Cord Network (SLSCoN) have supported the CBR programme for limited periods of time in specific places (WHO, 2013a; December 2017 field notes). In post-conflict areas, other NGOs, such as the Vanni Rehabilitation Organisation for the Differently-Abled (VAROD), have implemented active CBR programmes during and after the civil war that ended in 2009 (Chapter 5).

International organisations, including the WHO and the UNICEF, have played important roles in helping to shape and implement Sri Lanka's CBR policy, especially in the initial and development stages. In fact, one of the eight experts on the WHO's disability prevention and rehabilitation committee was Dr Padmani Mendis from Sri Lanka, who served as a member of the relevant advisory committee for over two decades from 1979 onwards (WHO, 1981). The impact of international actors on the shaping of policies related to CBR and disability issues is

---

[14] There are many possible reasons for inactive practices, such as difficulties in allocating one's own time to the activities, inadequate incentives, a lack of public recognition of CBR, and no continual training, amongst others. In addition, central government officers stated that they did not have any plans to conduct specific training sessions for community volunteers due to the development of self-help groups and the inactive functioning of the volunteers. However, they acknowledged that some volunteers have continued to conduct good practices at the grassroots level (December 2017 field notes).

discussed in the sections on process and content.

2.2. Context

This section discusses the multi-dimensional context. It notes the partnership between the government sector and the private sector, and touches upon the sociocultural context in Sri Lanka. It also explores the problems caused by the limited range of disability data available in the country.

Sri Lanka has introduced government-led systems, although the private sector has also been active in many arenas, as exemplified by the health and social welfare systems. According to some reports, Sri Lanka has created good health and welfare systems and has achieved relatively high results. These include lower infant and maternal mortality rates and a higher literacy rate than some other South Asian countries (McNay et al., 2004; Palafox 2011; Rannan-Eliya & Sikurajapathy, 2008). Early government investment in the health and social sectors, which was supported by external funding, such as contributions from international organisations and bilateral aid, created a foundation for the present system. Sri Lanka's CBR policy is a government-led initiative that cooperates with NGOs and DPOs, in alignment with the WHO's CBR guidelines (MSS, 2012a), although the CBR programme is not necessarily implemented or carried out in the same way as the majority of health and welfare systems, as discussed in the following sections.

At the grassroots level, indigenous knowledge, community support, traditional sociocultural phenomena, and religious activities provide a significant context that the actors, including local government sectors and NGOs, can incorporate into CBR practices (Miles 2002; Vasudevan, 2014). First, many mutual help activities and groups have been facilitated by government sectors within communities, although some of them have proved unsustainable and have re-developed by themselves. One of the most famous groups is the Women's Bank (Women's Bank of Sri Lanka, no date). A pilot project of women's mutual help groups was promoted by the National Housing Development Authority (NHDA) in the late 1980s. Community assistants were recruited by the NHDA, but some of them later became independent of the authority as they found it difficult to conduct mutual help activities within a governmental framework. They continued to develop these groups by themselves and established a cooperative bank. Building on the traditional community finance system of savings and credit and a microcredit scheme, the Women's Bank improved the members' own lives.

Second, Sri Lanka has diverse religions and ethnicities that have associations with development programmes. Approximately 74.9% of the total population is Sinhalese, the majority of whom are Theravada Buddhists, followed by Sri Lankan and Indian Tamils (15.6%) and Sri Lankan Moors (9.3%), amongst other groups (DCS, 2012). Although the literature reveals that some aspects of religion, including concepts of charity and Karma, can have a negative impact on the lives of disabled people (Liyanage, 2017), many actors incorporate religious and indigenous knowledge and activities into disability-inclusive development programmes, which is discussed in the section on content.

Third, traditional activities and indigenous knowledge remain prevalent in rural areas (Higuchi, 2002; Vasudevan, 2014). One example is 'Shramadana' which is also associated with religious thought and practice. 'Shramadana' is a system whereby local people share their labour and voluntarily give resources to other community members. The principle of 'Shramadana' and the philosophy of Mahatma Gandhi underpin the 'Sarvodaya' (සර්වෝදය) movement, which provides development programmes (Chandraratna, 1991; Perera, 1995). The Sarvodaya Suwasetha Sewa Society, for instance, initiated CBR programme in 1985 and has worked in cooperation with the national programme since 2003 (Sarvodaya Suwasetha Sewa Society Ltd., 2016).

Accurate and readily available data on disability issues in Sri Lanka remain limited (Weerasinghe & Jayatilake, 2015). In addition to disability statistics presented in Section 1.4, the Indian Ocean earthquake and tsunami in 2004 and the 26-year civil conflict were expected to cause many people to develop disabilities (Campbell, 2009; See also Chapter 5), but accurate data on war-related impairments are unavailable. Although the literature reveals an association between disability and poverty in the Sri Lankan context (Kumara & Gunewardena 2017; See also Chapter 4), reliable and valid data on disability issues and CBR achievements also remain limited (MSS, 2012a; December 2017 field notes). The problem of limited CBR data appears to be associated with a lack of monitoring and evaluation, as the following section discusses.

2.3. Process

As Table 3 (Section 1.4.) demonstrates, the situation of disability issues is linked to various events and legal systems, and are influenced by international actors. This section analyses the historical processes of CBR and its related sub-systems at the national level. It distinguishes between the following: 1) an interactive process with international norms in the 1980s; 2) a development process involving disability-related legal systems in the 1990s and 2000s; and 3) recent changes in the administration, budget allocation, and monitoring systems of CBR in the 2010s.

Pilot CBR projects officially commenced in Sri Lanka in the early 1980s. [15] The WHO's primitive CBR manual, which was partly

---

[15] According to Dr Padmani Mendis, interviewed on 5 January 2018, there were many

translated into Sinhalese, was tested in a rural area by two students from the Sri Lanka School of Social Work in 1981. A survey of child mental health problems was conducted within the primary healthcare system in 1982 (Herath, 2014; WHO, 1982). Another pilot project focussed on teacher training in the Anuradhapura and Kalutara districts in the early 1980s, and had received UNICEF's support since 1984 (UNICEF, 2003).[16] Together with some other events, such as a WHO interregional CBR consultation held in Colombo in 1982 (WHO, 1982), these interactive processes reveal the influence of international actors on the formation of Sri Lanka's CBR policy and practice.

Disability-related policies and regulations have been developed in Sri Lanka since the 1990s, as CBR became a national programme in the early 1990s. The efforts of disabled people, and particularly the National Council for Coordinating the Work of Disability Organizations,[17] led to the adoption of the Protection of the Rights of Persons with Disabilities Act in 1996 (Mendis, 1997). DPOs and other stakeholders, including Dr Mendis who chaired the drafting committee, helped to establish the National Policy on Disability in 2003. This policy states that CBR is 'a vehicle for the implementation of many strategies listed in this disability policy' (Ministry of Social Welfare, 2003: p. 33). Indeed, the national CBR programme covered all 25 districts of the country in 2014, with an increased coverage from 19 and 22 districts in 2002 and 2013 respectively (FIT, 2002; MSS, 2013; WHO, 2013a), although the National Action Plan for the Protection and Promotion of Human Rights

---

undocumented engagements by actors, including herself. For example, her engagement with NGOs, such as Sarvodaya, started in Sri Lanka in 1979.

[16] This is simply a description of the facts, but an in-depth evaluation is required. Some interviewees stated that UNICEF's engagement was unsuccessful because the main financial support was only provided to students. This led to a research-oriented approach without sufficient practice (December 2017 and January 2018 field notes).

[17] The National Council for Coordinating the Work of Disability Organizations was renamed and reorganised as the National Council for Persons with Disabilities in 1996. More than half of its members are required to be the disabled people appointed by the Minister.

pointed out the 'inadequate community-based rehabilitation programmes for people with disabilities' (Government of Sri Lanka, 2012: p. 128). Some other national frameworks and policies, such as Mahinda Chintana, a 10-year (2006–2016) national development plan (Ministry of Finance and Planning 2005, 2010), have provided financial assistance to low-income households with disabled members (Campbell, 2013).

In recent years, policy guidelines associated with the CBR programme have changed frequently. The name and structure of the ministry in charge of CBR changed from the 'Ministry of Social Services' in 2014 to the 'Ministry of Social Empowerment and Welfare' in 2016, and to the 'Ministry of Social Empowerment, Welfare, and Kandyan Heritage' in August 2017, and others. The current name is 'Ministry of Primary Industries and Social Empowerment' as of March 2019. Significantly, the competent authority for administering the CBR programme was demoted from the ministry level to the department level in 2014, with the potential loss of strong administrative power. According to an interview with a central government officer, the department sought to strengthen the relationship between provincial and central government officers in keeping with the government's decentralisation policy (December 2014 field notes). However, the department continued to maintain CBR's 'national' programme status in order to promote multisectoral implementation amongst ministries and investment by international organisations and donors (December 2017 field notes).

The recent budget allocated for the CBR programme has not changed drastically. Based on the ministry's annual reports from 2012 to 2017, approximately 2–5% of the annual budgetary provision was expected to be allocated to the CBR programme; this ranged from Rs. 7.7

million in 2012 to Rs. 13.3 million in 2015.[18] There are also other budgetary schemes for disabled people, such as a monthly allowance (Rs. 3,000) for low-income families with disabled members under the governmental development framework (Mahinda Chintana). The budgeted monthly allowance for this scheme, at Rs. 523.0 million in 2013 and Rs. 935.9 million in 2015, was larger than the CBR programme's budget. This indicates that the amount of direct financial welfare is significantly greater than that of the CBR.

The monitoring system still appears to be under development. The ministry and department responsible for social services has attempted to develop new systems, such as the CBR Management Information System (CBR MIS) in 2013 (WHO, 2013a), but this has not yet been implemented (December 2017 field notes). The draft national CBR plan for 2012–2016 included a plan for improving the monitoring system, and some monitoring committee meetings were held. However, the range of strategies available for monitoring and evaluating the impacts of CBR—for example, the impacts on promoting the participation of disabled people and on increasing the income of disabled people and their household members—appears to be undeveloped (MSS, 2012a).

2.4. Contents

The actual practice of CBR, as implemented by the actors at the macro, meso, and micro levels, has been influenced by the context and processes. An analysis of the content demonstrates that Sri Lanka's CBR programme is based on international frameworks, which is combined with indigenous knowledge and practical approaches in some divisions. The relationship between policy and practice is also discussed below,

---

[18] This included the allocated budget for the ministry, the NISD, the National Secretariat for Persons with Disabilities (NSPD), the Department of Social Services, and the National Secretariat for Elders. It excluded recurrent expenditure on other major and special programmes, and the budget of the Department of Divineguma Development.

with a focus on the similarities and differences between them.

The ministry responsible for social services has incorporated international CBR frameworks, including international disability norms (Campbell, 2011), into its policies and practical guidelines at the national level. The WHO's CBR manuals (e.g. Helander et al., 1980), for instance, were translated into Sri Lanka's national languages—Sinhalese and Tamil—and published by the ministry in cooperation with FRIDSRO. They were intended to train CBR stakeholders, such as community volunteers and SSOs. In addition, the CBR unit adopted the term 'CBID', which was introduced by the WHO et al. (2010), in some reports published after 2015. The ministry also attempted to integrate concepts found in the WHO's CBR guidelines and the World Report on Disability (WHO & World Bank, 2011) into the National Action Plan for Disability. This was supported by the WHO in the drafting process and approved by the Cabinet of Ministers in 2013 (MSS & Ministry of Health 2013; WHO 2016), although a lack of implementation has been observed (December 2017 field notes).

Data concerning the number of beneficiaries and the budget allocated for each activity reveals the content of the CBR programme at the national level. Table 4 presents the number of beneficiaries in 2013–2016, along with the national programme components. 'Home-based rehabilitation' has the largest number of beneficiaries on average, followed by 'referrals to physiotherapy services' and 'referrals to self-employment support'.

The content of the CBR programme at the district and divisional levels often differs from the central government's data concerning beneficiaries and budget allocations. For example, the SSOs reported on the monthly performance of CBR activities in the North-central Province. In a CBR model area in the province, a report written by an SSO, who was awarded the Anuradhapura district's Grand Prize in 2013/2014, emphasised the importance of community workshops ('Pantiya') and a religious programme to promote empowerment and inclusion (Chapters 6, 7, and 9).

This demonstrates that sociocultural and religious activities based on community relations have often been integrated into bottom-up practices at the divisional level. Community workshops have been developed by CBR stakeholders as a unique social investment activity in collaboration with the JOCVs in the Anuradhapura district, and have been included alongside the recommended CBR activities in that province (Chapter 7). The participants manufacture daily necessities, as an occupational activity, and sell these products in order to obtain a small income. The villagers support such activities and hold occasional events, some of which can be considered as 'Shramadana'(Figure 5). Similar community workshops have been launched and held in other districts (JSW's Report 2016; December 2017 field notes). Religious activities also appear to be common in grassroots CBR programmes across the country. For example, SSOs encourage disabled people to participate in religious activities, such as 'Sil samadan weema' (සිල් සමාදන් වීම), which is a common religious event for Theravada Buddhists (Chapters 4 and 9).

However, some SSOs and JSWs reported seeing almost no special CBR activities in certain rural areas (JSWs' reports from 2015 and 2016; 2015 field notes; December 2017 field notes). As noted in the section on the actors, in some divisions the CBR volunteers were registered but not given regular activities. The SSOs proceed with arrangements to provide welfare services—for example, by constructing a new house and providing a monthly allowance of Rs. 3,000 to low-income households with disabled members—yet some SSOs rarely conduct any community-based activities in their divisions.[19] The overall status of the activities implemented across the country has not been revealed, but one needs to consider the possibility that these policies may have lost their substance.

Table 4: The number of beneficiaries of the national CBR programme

	2013	2014	2015	2016	Average (2013–2016)
Home-based rehabilitation	6,427	6,743	8,121	5,571	6,716
Socialisation	1,414	2,074	2,543	1,935	1,992
Number of children referred to pre-schools	1,143	561	597	711	753
Number of children referred to schools	727	371	737	655	623
Number of children referred to special schools	991	538	694	629	713
Referrals to physiotherapy services	4,623	2,916	3,731	2,040	3,328
Referrals to vocational training	1,339	1,182	1,344	592	1,114
Referrals to employment opportunities	643	569	563	404	545
Referrals to self-employment support	2,725	2,138	2,573	1,077	2,128
Number of direct beneficiaries	114	55	309	101	145
Empowering Swashakthi (self-help) groups	17	744	378	1,136	569

Note: Adapted from Higashida (2018b). This table was created by the author using open documents from the government sector, including performance and progress reports from 2013 to 2016.

---

[19] This issue is related to the nature of social services, which are theoretically different from social work, especially in the Sri Lankan context (Subramaniam et al., 2014). Although the SSOs are expected to conduct community-based activities under the national CBR programme, their general responsibilities apart from CBR appear to provide direct social services for needy people.

Figure 5. Ground-breaking ceremony at a community workshop ('Pantiya') with disabled people, local government officers, and villagers, amongst others.

Note: I obtained the participants' permission to take and use this photo in July 2014.

Whilst the ministry and department responsible for social services have run the CBR programme in collaboration with NGOs, the activities of the NGOs appear to diverge from the governmental programme. For example, VAROD has conducted social investment programmes for disabled people in post-conflict areas in order to compensate for the lack of government livelihood support (WHO 2012; See also Chapter 5). It has used the micro-credit scheme and traditional customs to increase the household income of disabled people and their families, and has established and facilitated community rehabilitation committees (Chapter 5). Likewise, AKASA has implemented unique programmes, such as organising disabled women's groups, promoting advocacy in society, and conducting research on Sri Lankan disability issues (AKASA 2011; Campbell, 2009).

2.5. Discussion

This section summarises the study's main findings, revealing a complex set of dynamics between Sri Lanka's CBR policy and developmental social work practice, including its policy implementation gaps. It then discusses the challenges facing the CBR actors and the disability-related systems in Sri Lanka.

Main Findings: The Implementation of CBR

This study sought to reveal the relationship between policy at the national level and developmental social work practice at the community level in Sri Lanka's CBR programme. It has shed light on neglected aspects of policy implementation by using the policy analysis triangle and a relational approach. Focussing on the actors, context, processes, and content, the study has discovered a complex relationship between policy and practice, and has revealed the Sri Lankan approach to CBR. Whilst the country's CBR programme, which has been influenced by international norms and powerful actors, has been a government-led policy, the style of its approach appears to have been a synthesis of top-down implementation and bottom-up practices (Sabatier, 1986). For example, the ministry's reports on the beneficiaries of the CBR programme demonstrate the prioritisation of individual interventions, such as home-based rehabilitation and referrals to the social and health sections. By contrast, some stakeholders, such as SSOs, in the divisions have emphasised the importance of the bottom-up and collective programmes, including sociocultural and religious activities and social investment practices. This illustrates the synthesis between the national programme and bottom-up practices that mobilise local human resources and adopt indigenous approaches.

In addition to this approach, the context and processes in Sri Lanka suggest that the actors play a significant role in implementing and practicing CBR. The national programme was implemented by the MSS and the renamed ministries from the 1990s onwards. It uses international concepts, whilst NGOs have contributed to CBR in some rural areas. The administration responsible for the CBR programme was recently demoted from the ministry level to the department level, although it remains a national programme. Therefore, the current implementation of the CBR programme across the country depends on the efforts of local actors, such as the SSOs and other frontline officers, disabled people, and NGOs in each province, district, and division.

The findings also reveal some issues that affect CBR in Sri Lanka. This study observed implementation gaps, such as the underdeveloped system for developing human resources and the gap between the planned policy and the conducted practices. Indeed, the system of training and personnel allocation appeared underdeveloped. Some reports have also indicated that the CBR volunteers and SSOs are inactive at the grassroots level for multiple reasons, such as inadequate training and a lack of incentive. Although some disabled people have made an effort to promote their inclusion and empowerment, the extent to which disabled people have been encouraged to participate at the grassroots level across the country remains unclear. This uncertain situation is associated with another challenge, namely, the system of accurately monitoring and evaluating a programme that is still in the process of development.

Key Challenges Facing CBR: Focus on Actors

Based on these findings, this section discusses the challenges facing the actors in CBR and other disability-related systems in Sri Lanka. The key challenges include promoting the participation of disabled people, developing the capacity of human resources, and enhancing institutional functioning. These challenges are discussed both in relation to international concepts and in relation to local contexts.

The participation of disabled people in every aspect of development programmes is fundamental to the simultaneous achievement of empowerment and inclusion (Kuno & Seddon, 2003). In terms of the CBR programme, the involvement of disabled people and DPOs is crucial at the micro, meso, and macro levels (Rifkin & Kangare, 2002; WHO et al., 2010). Sri Lanka's government-led programme, including SSO's developmental social work activities, has worked to establish and support self-help groups, CBR steering committees, and national councils for disabled people, whilst the DPOs and the disabled people themselves have sought to promote inclusive systems (Mendis, 1997). These governmental commitments appear to reflect the national approach to promoting community development and mobilisation. There are, for instance, similar cases in which government sectors have promoted marginalised community groups, as happened in the case of the women's mutual help groups (Cassim et al., 1982; Women's Bank of Sri Lanka, no date). However, the substantial involvement of disabled people in planning, monitoring, and evaluating the CBR programme remains uncertain. Moreover, researchers have pointed out a similar issue, namely, the lack of any mechanism for implementing other disability-related acts (Campbell 2009, 2011; Liyanage, 2017). Although the conflict of interests between disabled people and the government actors, such as SSOs, may be the result of the government-led programme, I would

61

argue that policies based on the voices and involvement of the most marginalised disabled people and DPOs are needed, and must be promoted at every level of the CBR programme.

The stakeholders, in particular the government sector, faces the challenge of creating opportunities to develop the capacities of disabled people in order to achieve empowerment and inclusion in the local contexts. It is imperative to strengthen the systems of education and to provide essential staff to manage the CBR programme in order to promote the full participation of disabled people in society (Mendis, 1995). The main human resources in the CBR programme in Sri Lanka are the SSOs and the other frontline officers who play key roles in providing opportunities for disabled people's capacity development at the divisional level. The SSOs are not required to have specialised qualifications, such as a Bachelor's degree in Social Work, and they rarely receive related practical training or academic education. This is realistic given the limited number of officers with relevant educational and professional experience. There are, however, some challenges that should be addressed. Researchers argue that the NISD and other institutions should bridge the gaps between education and the provision of human resources in the field (Attanayake 2016; Subramaniam et al., 2014). In addition, strengthening Sri Lanka's educational and research systems in order to explore and develop its style of CBR and developmental social work could lead to significant differences from the internationally standardised or westernised approaches (Campbell, 2011; Herath, 2017). Although Sri Lanka may utilise international norms and frameworks, it is necessary to explore 'community-based' ('Prajaa muulika') practices with indigenous and context-specific approaches, which are exemplified by developmental, sociocultural and religious activities (Herath 2014; Herath 2017; Subramaniam et al., 2014; Vasudevan, 2014; See also Chapters 7, 8 and 9).

This indicates that capacity development is not only related to individuals, but also to institutions and systems (Hosono et al., 2011); therefore, the institutional capacity of the government sector, which includes adequate investments, is important in order to ensure sustainable and inclusive development (Asia Development Bank, 2005; Buse et al., 2012; Linder & Peters, 1989). Mendis (2016) suggests that the National Disability Commission (NDC) should be established within the president or prime minister's secretariat. This would be in keeping with the National Action Plan for Disability to promote inclusive policies, but it has not been realised. By contrast, for more than two decades, the national programme has been planned and implemented by the MSS and the renamed ministries, and the competent authority has been demoted to the Department of Social Services. The existing systems for implementing, monitoring, and evaluating the national CBR programme are unlikely to be sufficient or effective (MSS 2012a; December 2017 field notes). Given these circumstances, the national-level blueprint appears to be unclear. I therefore argue that a substantial and feasible CBR policy is required for further development, regardless of how many international stakeholders and powerful contributors are involved in Sri Lankan CBR. This would include a budget for promoting disabled people's participation, [20] improving the monitoring system, and strengthening the institutional capacity.

A partnership with other stakeholders is also essential for the actors. As the Department of Social Services promotes the multisectoral approach to CBR that is recommended worldwide (WHO, 2012; WHO et al., 2010), another key challenge involves promoting collaborative programmes between the various sectors. These include the ministries

---

[20] A provincial government sector responsible for social services in the North Central Province, for instance, has introduced a new policy to provide an allowance for disabled people who participate in community workshops in some divisions. This could be used to cover these participants' transportation costs in order to promote their participation (December 2017 field notes).

and departments related to education, health, employment, and transportation. [21] The government sector must also develop collaborations with NGOs that have conducted unique programmes, and have contributed to CBR and promoted the inclusion and empowerment of disabled people at the grassroots level. The sharing of knowledge and skills amongst these actors is another challenge that can potentially enhance disability-inclusive systems.

Previous Publication: This chapter is a revised version of my article: Higashida, M. (2018b). Relationship between the policy and practice of community-based rehabilitation: A case study from Sri Lanka. *Journal of Kyosei Studies, 2*, pp.1-31.

---

[21] Some good practices that address the challenges in Sri Lanka have been reported. The livelihood section of the CBR guidelines, for example, introduces the case of the Employers' Federation of Ceylon, which promotes employment opportunities for disabled people in collaboration with an international NGO (WHO et al., 2010).

CHAPTER THREE

Overview of Field Research Methodology

Drawing on the theoretical frameworks discussed in Chapter 1, this chapter presents the outline of the methodology of the research project in rural Sri Lanka. It includes research methods, field contexts, and my own positionality, as well as the overall process of the project. I emphasise the need for collaborative projects that include local stakeholders, including disabled people, whilst also underlining contextualisation, non-linear process, and pragmatism as essential concepts in these fields.

3.1. Methodology

This section shows the overall research methodology, which consists of quantitative and qualitative methods and practices in collaboration with local stakeholders. The methodology has been aligned with the study's aims, from a pragmatism perspective; it has also been aligned with the theoretical frameworks discussed in Chapter 1. Applied methods in each study area were selected flexibly, in line with the local contexts.

This research project was undertaken collaboratively with local stakeholders, including disabled people and SSOs in charge of CBR at the community level, to mainly explore the social reality of practices at a grassroots level (Sugiman, 2006) as well as disabled people's experiences (Mori et al., 2014). Surveys and interviews were conducted by CBR committee members, officers, and other stakeholders related to CBR, including the author.

This research project used mixed methods—a quantitative survey and a qualitative study—with practices in rural community settings to expand the range of data analysis (Greene et al., 1989). The mixed-methods approach is often controversial because it can include different paradigms simultaneously, such as positivism in quantitative studies and social constructionism in some qualitative studies (Johnson et al., 2007). This project used pragmatism to examine practical and useful knowledge in society through a mixed-methods approach (Feilzer, 2010).

The actual methods, including a quantitative survey using scales, group and individual interviews, participant observation, and policy analysis, were selected in line with the objectives of the studies and needs revealed through dialogue with local stakeholders in each study area. For triangulation (Mertens & Hesse-Biber, 2012; O'Leary, 2005), my field diary was also utilised to confirm meanings in local contexts. One of the main methods applied was using semi-structured interviews to collect narrative data of the disabled people. To encourage the research participants to express their experiences openly, the research team asked questions based on the basic structure and main topics.

Narrative and qualitative data were analysed by thematic analysis (Guest et al., 2011; Kawakita, 1967). NVivo software was used for qualitative analysis in some studies (Chapters 4 and 5). Although each study had a different procedure, the basic procedures consisted of the following six steps: 1) transcribing narrative data using the handwritten and voice recorder data, 2) loading the narrative data into NVivo or putting the transcribed data onto sticky notes, 3) reading the transcript data carefully, 4) coding each sentence in line with similar meanings, and generating categories based on meanings and exploring common themes, 5) searching the relationships between codes and themes, and 6) drawing relationships amongst categories.

3.2. Field Sites and Positionality

Because of the complex contexts this project involved, it was necessary to describe the background, field characteristics, and my own positionality during the project. After commencing work in a local government office as an international social worker in February 2013, I began to apply some research methods. As presented in Table 5, the project consists of several periods between 2013 and 2018.[22] Each study area had unique contexts and my positionality in each field was different, as follows.

The first site was in the M-division (pseudonym) of the Gampaha district, Western Province; research was carried out from May to July 2016, in December 2017, and in April 2018. The main placement organisation was the social services section of the DS, in collaboration with local NGOs. Although the social services section of the M-division implemented the CBR programme, the situation was quite likely to be under development. As a researcher, I was mainly in charge of the research project on the socioeconomic participation of disabled youth. I spoke only Sinhalese in the division during the field project.

---

[22] In addition to three main study sites, complementary studies were conducted during the periods in other areas, including Colombo in the Western Province, Kandy in the Central Province, Trincomalee in the Eastern Province, and the Southern Province.

Table 5: Basic information of the research project in Sri Lanka

	District	Main Study Site	Study Period	Placement Sector	Positionality
1	Gampaha	M-division	May 2016–Jul 2016	Government/	Researcher
			Dec 2017	NGO	
			Apr 2018		
2	Mullaitivu	(all divisions)	Jan 2016–Oct 2016	NGO	Consultant
			Jan 2018		
3	Anuradhapura	R-division	Jan 2013–Jan 2015	Government	International social worker, Researcher
			Dec 2017–Jan 2018		
			Apr 2018		

Note: This table was created by the author.

The second site was in Mullaitivu district, consisting of five divisions in the Northern Province. This was a conflict-affected area during the 26-year armed civil war. Stakeholders of the project, including myself, began to contact stakeholders and discuss the project in January 2016. In May 2016, I visited for the first time an NGO that conducted a CBR programme in the Vanni, including social investment activities in Mullaitivu District. We carried out the research project in October 2016 and January 2018, whilst I took the initiative in the project on site as an individual consultant. I spoke English, and the NGO staff translated my comments from English into the Tamil language.

The third site was in rural areas of Anuradhapura district in the North-central Province; research was carried out from February 2013 to January 2015, from December 2017 to January 2018, and in April 2018. The R-division (pseudonym) in the Anuradhapura district was a model area for the national CBR programme. I worked as a social worker from 2013 to 2015 in the social services section of the DS in R-division, whilst participating in various local activities in the CBR programme. In addition to the R-division, other divisions in the district were also research targets, based on the model practice in the R-division. The participation opportunities included CBR steering committees, community workshops, home visits, key stakeholder meetings, events related to disability issues, and research programmes. In particular, community workshops, which constitute a social investment programme, were one of the key CBR practices in the region (See Chapter 6). Since the end of the social work activities, I have been involved as a researcher. I spoke only Sinhalese in the division during the field project.

3.3. Process in Each Field: Non-linear Process and Dynamics

The process in the project involved a 'non-linear pattern of planning, acting, observing, and reflecting on the changes in the social situations' (Noffke & Stevenson, 1995: p. 2). In this research project, it was important to flexibly consider the next step and strategy in line with needs and changes in local circumstances.

As presented in Table 6, the stages of the project could be divided into situation analysis, planning and design, implementation and monitoring, and evaluation based on CBR guidelines (WHO et al., 2010). However, the process appears to have been neither simple nor linear. This is partly because I commenced activities in the middle of the

69

ongoing programme. For example, it was necessary to observe the existing activities at an early stage in Anuradhapura district. Additionally, one activity had an impact on other activities during the process. Identifying the situation of participation and building networks around educational issues, for instance, was done through reflection after observation. Hence, I argue that such complex processes are a field reality, in line with field contexts. I discuss these issues whilst reflecting on field experiences and positionality at the grassroots level in Section 10.2.

Table 6: Theme and process of the research project in each area

	District	Study Site	Theme of Activity/Action	Process
1	Gampaha	M-division	• Socioeconomic participation • Socioeconomic barriers	1-1) Situation analysis
2	Mullaitivu	(all divisions)	• Participation and livelihood • Disabled people's organisation	2-1) Situation analysis 2-2) Planning and design
3	Anuradhapura	R-division	• Developing local resources • Community mobilisation • Multisectoral approach in education	3-1) Situation analysis and evaluation 3-2) Planning and design 3-3) Implementation and monitoring 3-4) Situation analysis, planning and design, and implementation 3-5) Monitoring and evaluation

Note: This table was created by the author.

70

3.4. Social Context in Each Project Site

This section organises and presents basic information about the sites, including descriptive disability and population statistics based on official data. It points out the unique aspects, such as contexts and potential needs, from the perspective of promoting the participation of disabled people.

The prevalence of impairments at the district level is unclear, according to existing data. Table 7 presents the proportion of the type of impairment in these districts (DCS, 2001), although it has several limitations. The percentage of each disability is within the following range: from 1.39% in Gampaha to 1.99% in Anuradhapura. As recent official data has not been available since 2001, this census could be quite different from the current situation. Data in the conflict-affected areas, including Mullaitivu District, was excluded from the census. In addition, intellectual and psychiatric impairments were mixed into the statistics. By contrast, the ESCAP report (2015) shows a disability prevalence of 8.7% based on Sri Lankan government-reported data.[23] However, this data does not include the prevalence at the district level. Because of the various classifications of impairments or disabilities, the DCS (2001) and ESCAP (2015) data are not comparable. Hence, I argue that data collection at the grassroots level is necessary to reveal the local situation in the country.

Regarding socioeconomic contexts, including ethnic diversity, Table 8 illustrates the different aspects at three study sites. Whilst the Sinhalese are the ethnic majority in the Gampaha and Anuradhapura districts, constituting more than 90% of the population, particularly in the R-division (100%), Tamils are the majority in the Mullaitivu district

---

[23] The world health survey shows the estimated disability prevalence of 12.9% in Sri Lanka (WHO, 2011a).

(88%), according to governmental census data (DCS, 2012).

The distinctive features in industries and employment in each study site are identified by the comparison of the national average and the megacity, Colombo. According to data of the DCS (2018), the features of the Gampaha district is relatively similar to Colombo, whereas those of the Anuradhapura district and the Mullativu district are likely to be similar compared with Colombo. In terms of the share of population employed by three major industry groups, namely agriculture, industries and services, the Gampaha district has the rate in services at 58.4% and that in agriculture at 3.2% in 2017. The rate of population in agriculture is the higher in the Anuradhapura district and the Mullativu district, having more than 40%. Regarding the employment status, 'own account worker' in 'self-employed' persons is the highest in the Anuradhapura district and the Mullaitivu district with more than 40%, although the Anuradhapura district has a distinctive rate of 'contributing family worker' at 18.9%. The unemployment rate in the Anuradhapura district and the Mullaitivu district is more than 4%, but that in the Gampaha district at 3.3 is lower than Colombo and the national average.

The economic conditions are likely to be different for these groups. Figure 6 presents poverty rates estimated by the DCS (2015, 2017), based on the official poverty line. One of the distinctive features of Mullaitivu District is that it has the highest poverty rate in Sri Lanka, at 28.8% (±2.5%) in 2012/2013, and the second highest rate at 12.7% in 2016. Amongst the three districts, the second highest poverty rate is in Anuradhapura District, at 7.6% (±1.1%) in 2012/2013 and 3.8% in 2016. The Gampaha district is at 2.1% (±0.3%), which is still higher than the megacity, Colombo, at 1.4% (±0.3%) in 2012/2013 and 2.0 in 2016. The M-division (6.0%) is the second-highest division in the Gampaha district in 2012/2013. The figure therefore suggests that these features in each district should be considered when analysing the socioeconomic aspects of disability issues such as participation and earning a living.

As presented above, each field site appears to have a unique context. The WHO et al. (2010) said that 'many different needs will have been identified during Stage 1 [situation analysis] which could all potentially be addressed by a CBR programme. Unfortunately, resources are not unlimited, and therefore priorities will need to be set' (p. 48). It is therefore necessary to consider the socioeconomic, cultural, and religious contexts of research projects involving CBR.

Table 7: Population-based proportion by type of impairment in study sites at the district level

	Total	Visual	Speech/ Hearing	Hands	Mobility	Other physical impairment	Mental impairment
Gampaha	1.39%	0.34%	0.38%	0.25%	0.48%	0.07%	0.35%
Mullaitivu	N/A	N/A	N/A	N/A	N/A	N/A	N/A
Anuradhapura	1.99%	0.52%	0.50%	0.34%	0.67%	0.10%	0.40%
Sri Lanka (18 Districts)[1]	1.63%	0.41%	0.44%	0.29%	0.54%	0.08%	0.41%

Notes: Data were retrieved from DCS (2001) based on the Census of Population and Housing.
[1]Northern and Eastern Provinces, including the Mullaitivu district, are excluded from the census.

Table 8: Population and ethnic group proportion in study sites at the district level

	Population in thousands (2016)[1]	Proportion by ethnic group (2012)[2]			
		Sinhalese	Tamils (Sri Lankan and Indian)	Moors (Sri Lankan and Indian)	Other[3]
Gampaha District	2,372	90.5%	3.9%	4.2%	1.3%
M-division (in Gampaha District)	164	94.7%	1.7%	3.4%	0.2%
Mullaitivu District	95	9.7%	88.2%	2.0%	0.1%
Anuradhapura District	905	91.0%	0.6%	8.2%	0.2%
R-division (in Anuradhapura District)	33	100.0%	0.0%	0.0%	0.0%
Sri Lanka (Country)	21,203	74.9%	15.3%	9.3%	0.5%

Source:
1. Mid-year Population Estimates by District and Sex, 2012-2016 (DCS, 2016)
2. Census of Population and Housing of Sri Lanka, 2012 (DCS, 2012)
3. Burgher, Malay, Sri Lanka Chetty, Bharatha, and others

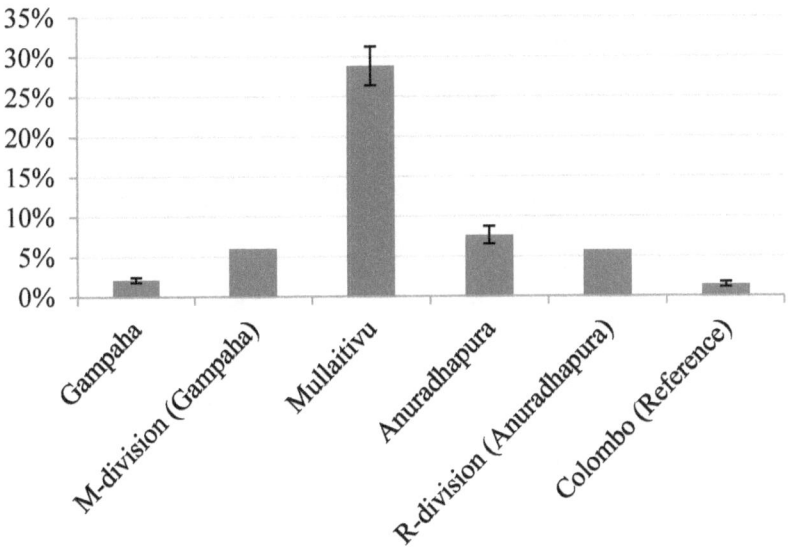

Figure 6. Estimated poverty rates under Sri Lanka's official poverty line in the study sites

Notes: Data were retrieved from DCS (2015) based on the Household Income and Expenditure Survey in 2012/2013. The standard error is not available in the M-division and R-division.

3.5. Ethical Considerations

This research project was approved by the Research Ethics Review Committees at the relevant academic institutions, including the University of Sheffield (reference number: 007919) and Osaka University (reference number: OUKS1745), making an agreement with governmental institutions and NGOs in Sri Lanka.

After information on the research study was provided in the research participants' native Sinhalese or Tamil languages, written and/or verbal consent was also obtained from them. They were assured that refusal to be interviewed would have no impact on them. Family caregivers who helped a disabled person on a regular basis were asked to participate and to consent concerning participation of the disabled person. Simultaneously, the interviewee's consent was obtained for recording the semi-structured interviews. Consent was sought on an ongoing basis.

CHAPTER FOUR

Situation Analysis In A Pilot Area

As the capability approach indicates, not only capability inputs—resources and commodities—but also personal, social and environmental conversion factors are likely to be crucial factors in terms of the socioeconomic participation of disabled people. In particular, socioeconomic participation of disabled youth is affected by the multiple conversion factors and also 'within the household dynamics' (Braithwaite & Mont, 2009: p. 222). Because disabled youth may have to rely on the household's income and family member's conditions (Filmer, 2008; WHO, 2007), it is necessary to consider the impact of conversion factors at the household level, including poverty transitions (Grech, 2015; Shahtahmasebi et al., 2011), on participation.

In terms of the conversion factors at the household level, it is important to distinguish the positionality between the disabled youth and other household members. According to the family model of disability, which complements the social model of disability (Kuno, 2012; Kuno & Seddon, 2003), family members also experience 'disability' because of the social inequality associated with disabled people. Family caregivers face limitations in their own lives due to the economic, physical, and psychosocial burden of nursing care and personal assistance (Brett, 2002; Grech, 2015). However, these family members also have different positionalities, experiences, and views than those of disabled people, which can often present a conflict of interests (Kuno, 2012; Kuno & Seddon, 2003).

The objective of this situation analysis is to examine the association of socioeconomic participation of disabled youth with conversion factors at the household and individual levels in M-division, Gampaha district. This project includes the following research questions:

1. To what extent and how do disabled youth participate in socioeconomic activities in a rural area?

2. To what extent and how do conversion and related factors at the household and individual levels affect the socioeconomic participation of disabled youth?

Mixed methods, which consisted of quantitative and qualitative research, were applied. First, a survey was conducted through in-home interviews with disabled youth (n = 116). Statistical analysis, including multiple regression, was employed to identify significant conversion factors that contributed to socioeconomic participation. Second, semi-structured interviews with disabled youth (n = 26) and their caregivers in deprived households were implemented amongst the nested sample of the survey. The narrative data were analysed by thematic analysis.

4.1. The Extent of Achieved Socioeconomic Participation

Demographic and Other Variables

Table 9 includes the basic characteristics of the disabled youth participants and variables of conversion factors and capability inputs in the quantitative study. The age of the research participants of disabled youth ranged from 15 to 29 years with an average age of 22.1 ± 5.4 years. The majority of participants had an intellectual or developmental impairment (44.0%), followed by physical (22.4%) and psychiatric impairments (10.3%). The mean of the extent of impairment/activity-limitation assessed partly using the WHO Disability Assessment Schedule (WHO-DAS-II: WHO, 2010), which was standardised from 0–100, was 49.0 ± 15.8.

In terms of variables of capability inputs and conversion factors, the median household monthly income was Rs. 15,000 per month, and 44.0% earned less than Rs. 12,400, which was below the poverty line for a typical family (WageIndicator.org, 2016; World Bank, 2015). In addition, 62.1% of the households reported hardship in their everyday lives. With regard to those variables at the individual level, the average monthly income of the disabled youth was Rs. 1205.2 per month, and 94.0% of them earned Rs. 4,094 or below. In addition, 17.2% of the disabled youth received a social welfare allowance (Rs. 3,000) from the government sector, whilst only 37.1% reported that they were aware of any activities of the CBR programme. Whereas 58.6% of the disabled youth participants had attended school for at least two years, 29.3% had no experience of learning at any institution in mainstream or special education classes.

Table 9: Relationships between socioeconomic participation and other multiple variables

Variable	Category	Option		Value[a]		P-value
Demographic variables	Age	(years)	22.1±5.4	-0.09	n.s.	0.316
	Gender	Male	49.1%	1.08 (±0.19)	n.s.	0.077
		Female	50.9%	1.02 (±0.18)		
	Ethnicity	Sinhalese	92.2%	1.04 (±0.19)	n.s.	0.201
		Others (Moor and Tamil)	7.8%	1.13 (±0.17)		
	Marital status	Unmarried	93.1%	1.04 (±0.18)	*	0.010
		Married	6.9%	1.26 (±0.13)		
Household-level variables	Household size	(people)	4.3±1.3	-0.07	n.s.	0.431
	Education level of parents (highest)	Grade ≦ 5	13.8%	0.95 (±0.17)	n.s.	0.570
		Grade 6-12	68.1%	1.06 (±0.19)		
		Grade ≧ 13	18.1%	1.08 (±0.16)		
	Employment status	Unemployed	13.8%	1.01 (±0.15)	n.s.	0.817
		Employed	34.5%	1.06 (±0.21)		
		Self-employment	45.7%	1.05 (±0.18)		
		Pension/inheritance	6.0%	1.05 (±0.16)		
	Household monthly income (except for allowance)	< Rs.12,400	44.0%	1.00 (±0.16)	**	0.009
		Rs.12,400-29,376	40.5%	1.11 (±0.19)		
		> Rs.29,376	15.5%	1.05 (±0.20)		
	Allowance (Samurdhi)	Yes	50.9%	1.07 (±0.18)	n.s.	0.164
		No	49.1%	1.03 (±0.19)		
	Hardship (household)	Yes	62.1%	1.00 (±0.18)	***	<0.001
		No	37.9%	1.11 (±0.17)		
	Owned additional field/firm	Yes	12.9%	1.11 (±0.17)	n.s.	0.176
		No	87.1%	1.04 (±0.19)		
	Mountainous area	< 100m	85.3%	1.06 (±0.19)	n.s.	0.528
		≧ 100m	14.7%	1.02 (±0.19)		
Variables of the disabled youth	Educational experiences	< 2 years	41.4%	0.93 (±0.14)	***	<0.001
		≧ 2 years	58.6%	1.14 (±0.16)		
	Monthly income of disabled youth	< Rs.3,000	77.6%	1.04 (±0.17)	n.s.	0.131
		≧ Rs.3,000	22.4%	1.10 (±0.23)		
	Social welfare allowance	Yes	17.2%	1.00 (±0.20)	n.s.	0.251
		No	82.8%	1.06 (±0.18)		
	Have you met a social services officer? (having met a social services officer)	Yes	45.7%	1.09 (±0.19)	*	0.044
		No	54.3%	1.02 (±0.18)		
	Do you know a CBR programme in the division? (information about CBR)	Yes	37.1%	1.13 (±0.19)	**	0.001
		No	62.9%	1.01 (±0.17)		
(Impairment/ activity-limitation variables)	WHO-DAS-II (8 items)	(Log-transformed)	1.18±0.13	-0.60	***	<0.001
	Type of impairment	Intellectual/development	44.0%	1.00 (±0.16)	***	<0.001
		Physical	22.4%	1.12 (±0.18)		
		Psychiatric	10.3%	1.07 (±0.09)		
		Deaf-mute	7.8%	1.21 (±0.18)		
		Multiple	15.5%	0.94 (±0.17)		

Note: Adapted from Higashida (2017b). The summary score of the log-transformed socioeconomic participation variables was entered as the dependent variable. [a]The value of each independent variable shows the means of socioeconomic participation (log-transformed), except for the correlation rates for age, household size and WHO-DAS-II score (log-transformed); *p<0.05, **p<0.01, ***p<0.001, n.s.=no significant difference. There was a significant association between household monthly income and hardship, and socioeconomic participation at the household level; participants who lived in a disadvantaged household with a low-level income and hardship had lower levels of socioeconomic participation than those living in an advantaged household with a higher income and no hardship. The means ± SD of the log-transformed socioeconomic participation variables were 1.00 ± 0.16, 1.11 ± 0.19 and 1.05 ± 0.20 for a household below the poverty line (<Rs. 12,400), one had a less-than-median income (Rs.12,400–29,376) and one had a higher income (>Rs. 29,376), respectively ($F(2, 113)=4,88$, $p=0.009$).

Extent of socioeconomic participation

This analysis shows the current degree of archived socioeconomic participation of disabled youth participants, which was assessed using questions that were extracted from the CBR indicators (WHO, 2015). The mean ± SD of the sum of socioeconomic participation in all six components—with learning, work, culture/religion, recreation/sports, voting, and community group—was 2.1 ± 0.9, where 1 and 5 were allocated to the lowest ('not at all') and highest ('completely') scores, respectively. The summed rates of 'not at all' and 'a little' in all items was 70.3%. In terms of each level of socioeconomic participation, more than 50% of the disabled youth reported 'not at all' or 'a little' for all of the components. The means ± SD ranged from 1.7 ± 1.2 in the 'community group' to 2.6 ± 1.1 for 'culture/religion'.

The association between multiple factors and achieved socioeconomic participation

After adjusting the data for statistical analysis, this analysis presents the association of socioeconomic participation with independent variables (Table 9). There was a significant association between socioeconomic participation and eight independent variables: demographic variable (marital status), household-level variables (household monthly income and hardship), variables of the disabled youth (educational experiences, having met a social services officer, and having information about CBR), and two impairment/activity-limitation variables (WHO-DAS-II and type of impairment).

A significant association between socioeconomic participation and the conversion factors in the disabled youth was observed. Participants who had at least two years of educational experiences had higher socioeconomic participation scores than those who had less than two years of school attendance. The means ± SD of log-transformed socioeconomic participation scores were 1.14 ± 0.16 and 0.93 ± 0.14 for educational experiences of two or more years and for those of less than two years, respectively (t(114)=-7.235, p<0.001). In addition, the socioeconomic participation scores of participants who had met an SSO and obtained information about CBR were significantly higher than the scores of those who had not. The socioeconomic participation scores were 1.09 ± 0.19 for those who had met an SSO and 1.02 ± 0.18 for those who had not (t(114)=-2.04, p=0.044), and they were 1.13 ± 0.19 for those with CBR information and 1.01 ± 0.17 for those with information about CBR (t(114)=-3.58, p=0.001).

Multiple regression analysis of achieved socioeconomic participation

This multiple regression analysis reveals the association of socioeconomic participation with the conversion factors, after adjusting data statistically and controlling for the effect of demographic and impairment/activity-limitation variables (Table 10). The following conversion factors had a significant association with the socioeconomic participation of disabled youth: two or more years of educational experience, hardship and information about CBR. Amongst the conversion factors in the second model, the most significant predictor of

82

socioeconomic participation was previous educational experience (β=0.34, p<0.001), followed by hardship (β=-0.19, p=0.005) and information about CBR (β=0.16, p=0.012). Therefore, participants who had more than two years of educational experience, lived in a household without hardship, and had obtained information about CBR had significantly higher socioeconomic participation scores.

4.2. Experiences of Socioeconomic Participation

This qualitative study based on semi-structured interviews explored the experiences of socioeconomic participation of disabled youth and conversion factors, including the social barriers and facilitators, amongst deprived households (n = 26). In line with the two research questions, two main categories were generated: 'current lifestyle with socioeconomic participation' and 'social barriers and facilitators'. I argue that the complex dynamics of social barriers, including the phenomenon of the marginalisation of disabled youth within the household, influenced socioeconomic participation of disabled youth, though family caregivers also suffered from the hardship.

Table 10: The association between socioeconomic participation and conversion factors

	Model 1		Model 2	
Educational experiences	0.48	**	0.34	**
Hardship	-0.23	**	-0.19	**
Information about CBR	0.20	**	0.16	*
Impairments/activity-limitations			-0.39	**
Marital status			0.16	*
R^2	0.41		0.59	

$**p < .01, *p < .05$

Notes: Adapted from Higashida (2017b). Data are standardised regression coefficients (β). Socioeconomic participation (log-transformed) scores were entered as the dependent variable. Impairment/activity-limitation was assessed using the WHO-DAS-II (log-transformed). Educational experiences, hardship, information about CBR and marital status were entered as dichotomous variables (0 = no; 1 = yes).

Current lifestyle with socioeconomic participation

This category showed types of socioeconomic participation in each individual life. It consisted of three themes: 'almost nothing', 'using institutions', and 'work in the community'. First, the disabled youth participants who spent time at home without any outside social activities were identified ('almost nothing'). For example, the sister of a female participant (no. 25) stated, 'She spends all her time at home, but she is good at housekeeping, like cleaning and washing....She doesn't participate in such [community] activities'. Some of them did not even have their own identification (ID) card, which is necessary for public procedures as a resident, such as voting; this phenomenon was also reported in another province (Association of Women with Disabilities [AKASA], 2011). A mother of a male participant (no. 20) described his condition as follows: 'He doesn't participate in any activities....I haven't made his ID card because he doesn't need one'.

However, many disabled youth, even those who did not have a regular opportunity, participated in cultural and religious activities held at places close to their homes. In particular, religious participation seemed to be important for villagers, including disabled people, in Sri Lanka. A female participant (no. 4) stated that she went to a Buddhist temple for 'Sil gannawa' (සිල් ගන්නවා) or 'Sil samadan weema' (සිල් සමාදන් වීම) on every full moon day, which is a basic religious occasion for Theravada Buddhists (Figure 7).

Second, several participants utilised educational and vocational training institutions for disabled youth in the community ('using institutions'). These institutions provided many opportunities for their socioeconomic participation, including education and vocational training as well as cultural and religious activities, which involved social interaction with others outside their homes. A female student with an intellectual impairment (no. 5) who attended a special needs education class showed certifications she had earned at sports and cultural events, stating: 'I got them. I'm happy'.

Third, some disabled youth in this study had high-level opportunities for socioeconomic participation ('work in the community'). Their main participation opportunities included a peer-supporter, community work, and self-employment (Figure 8), and they were likely to participate in other activities, such as religious events, the memorial services of villagers, and community group activities such as self-help groups. A peer-supporter (no. 24) of an institution for disabled people explained his life with participation:

Figure 7. 'Sil samadan weema' for disabled youths and children

Note: I obtained the participants' permission to take and use this photo in 2016.

Figure 8. Self-employment at a retail shop ('Kade')

Note: I obtained the participants' permission to take and use this photo in 2016.

Since graduating from this centre [training], I
have worked as a peer-supporter. I can't do
detailed work because of my impaired hands, but

86

I'm in charge of assisting other staff and taking
care of disabled children here....I'm satisfied
with my life.

One of the participants, however, was potentially deprived through his work in the community. The sister of a male participant with an intellectual impairment (no. 26) described the situation:

He often goes outside to cut coconuts....Some
villagers come to our house, and they invite him
to do so....Basically, workers should receive a
wage, like Rs. 50–60 per coconut tree, but he just
works without being paid. Those villagers use
him as a means of their own benefits.

This case indicates the importance of the context and method of participation, even if the disabled youth take part in activities in the community.

Social barriers and facilitators

Main themes and subthemes were derived from the narrative data, which were encompassed by the broad theme of 'social barriers and facilitators'. The main themes were as follows: 1) previous educational and vocational experiences, 2) household economic conditions, 3) personal assistance by caregivers, and 4) perceived resource information and sociocultural image. I outline varied facilitators and barriers to socioeconomic participation. In addition, I argue that social barriers, including low-prioritisation and marginalisation of disabled youth's participation at the household level, are crucial, although household members also suffered from low-income and hardship.

Previous educational and training experiences

This subtheme is comprised of 'no experience', 'short-term participation', and 'continuity', which indicates a gap in participation level. Some of the disabled youth participants had 'no experiences' for socioeconomic participation in their lives. In particular, those who had no educational or training experiences tended to stay home all the time. The typical case was exemplified by the narrative of a mother of a male youth with an intellectual impairment (no. 21): 'He has never attended school in his life. He is always at home....He plays with our other children at home'.

Even if disabled youth begin to participate in education and training, it does not necessarily mean that they will continue them or that they will have any further opportunity ('short-term participation'). The mother of a daughter (no. 2) who attended a class stated:

Yes, she did [attend a school] for one year. But it felt meaningless because the teacher didn't teach students well. So I stopped taking her to the school....Since then, she has stayed home. Actually, she doesn't like to participate in such things now.

In addition, the mother of a son (no. 3) explained that he had no socioeconomic participation after cancellation of a school: 'Yeah, we tried to take him to a school for four months, but we had to cancel it....Now, we aren't looking for any other opportunities for him'. Whilst these cases included the positionality and experiences of the caregiver, the account indicates that negative experiences and a period without any socioeconomic participation led to difficulties in finding new opportunities because the household members and the disabled youth became accustomed to their lives without them.

Those who had participated in education and vocational training were likely to have further opportunities for socioeconomic participation ('continuity'). One of the straight pathways was narrated by the father of a youth who had multiple impairments (no.14):

He went to a normal [mainstream] school for a bit but could not follow the class....After staying at an educational institution for the disabled for eight years, he received vocational training at a training centre and learned how to make cloth-wicks ('Pahan tiraya'/පහන් තිරය). [This is used when chanting a sutra.]

His son, the disabled youth, also explained: 'Using this machine that I received from the centre, I make and sell cloth-wicks in a town'. Additionally, a youth with an intellectual disability (no. 5) participated in education, although she was moved from a mainstream school to a school for special needs education. Her mother said she became familiar with participation not only in learning but also in other activities, such as dance performance in front of an audience. She said: 'Yes. I like to dance'.

However, receiving training and education do not necessarily lead to further participation. For instance, the mother of a female participant (no.

6) who attended a special needs education class and rehabilitation at a centre mentioned the discontinuity:

She went to some institutions, but now she just stays at home. She does not do anything or participate in any activities. She just does small things like housework.

Household economic conditions

Economic conditions at the household level impacted the socioeconomic participation of the disabled youth. This subtheme consisted of 'low household income and hardship' and 'additional costs' that were associated with the socioeconomic participation of these individuals. I argue that the significant point concerns the dynamics at the household level based on these economic conditions.

The majority of caregivers reported the severity of their 'low-level household income and hardship'. These barriers along with another subtheme ('additional costs') led to the limitation of the disabled youth's participation. The representative and simple answer as to why their participation was limited was stated by a mother (no. 16): 'The reason is just the economic problems of our household'.

The father of another participant (no. 8) explained a story regarding the changes in his livelihood. He stated that he was satisfied with a job at his retail shop before the birth of his son. However, he had to close up his shop because he was no longer able to run it due to the excessive burden to provide nursing care for the disabled son. He said: 'We are just struggling.... The only thing that we can do now is to live with these severe conditions somehow'.

The low-level household income conditions and hardships are barriers that impact the participation of disabled youth through their marginalisation. From the viewpoint of the heads of household who support the family financially, some of them could not avoid prioritising their own livelihood. An illustrative narrative was stated by a mother (no. 16):

If we take her anywhere, nobody in this family can work and earn money because both of us [mother and father] must go with her. She needs constant attendance of us for moving due to her legs [impairments].

In addition, there were disabled youth who had to change their living style due to the severe household conditions. A disabled youth (no. 13), for example, considered terminating a vocational training programme before its completion due to household financial problems, although he liked to be trained at the centre. These cases indicate the marginalisation of disabled youth in households with a disadvantaged status, whilst family members also struggle with hardships in their lives.

'Additional costs' or consumption needs for the disabled youth were also often required, which could be barriers to the socioeconomic participation of the disabled youth. These costs included transportation costs and medical bills, which were directly and indirectly related to the process of their participation. Although some participants tried to overcome their difficulties, the additional costs were negative factors for the majority of the participants.

First, transportation costs would be one of the most direct and critical issues of their socioeconomic participation. If the disabled youth and their household members decided to participate in any activities held in locations that were not approachable on foot, using public transportation was a potential option for them. Bus and train services were available for residents whose houses were close to a bus stop or train station. Most participants, however, had at least one condition that made it difficult for them to utilise the relatively affordable transportation. In such cases, a 'three-wheel', which is a hired individual transportation service called 'Tuk-Tuk' in some Asian countries, was likely to be the sole option. One of the most typical narratives was stated by a father of a disabled youth (no. 3) who had attended a special need education class; this account also illustrated the relationship between transportation and previous educational experiences:

He went to the class with his mother by bus, but we could no longer take him to the school. It was quite difficult for us to take him by bus because his weight became too heavy to hold in our arms. After that, we had to hire a three-wheel to take him anywhere outside. But it is much more expensive, like Rs. 500 for a round-trip by a three-wheel, whereas it only takes Rs. 48 for the same route by bus. We had no choice but to stop it.

Some household members, however, tried to handle the difficulties by adjusting the frequency with which they participated in an activity. A mother (no. 5) explained an alternative strategy to solve these issues:

Although we usually come here by hired
three-wheel, we came here by a small van today.
I discussed the expensive transportation problem
with other parents recently, and we decided to
try a school van as a test, which other school
students usually use.

These episodes might include other themes, such as 'personal assistance by caregivers', but it can be said that the additional costs affected their participation and the process of the household's decisions.

Second, other costs had an indirect relationship with the socioeconomic participation of the disabled youth. In particular, medical bills influenced a household's decision about the disabled youth's participation. Most household members reported high additional costs at pharmacies or private hospitals.[24] The mother of a daughter who had an intellectual impairment and epilepsy (no. 2), for example, explained the expensive costs of medication for her:

We have paid Rs. 7,000 for drugs for her
bimonthly, and it is too expensive. Most of our
costs for her are spent on prescriptions. We never
have any money left over.

This narrative indicates that medical treatment was inevitably

---

[24] Although public hospitals provide basic and free medical consultations and treatments for all and the government sector provides some medical assistance, in some cases, patients have to pay for any related expenses. Because of the higher necessity for medical treatment and rehabilitation to treat impairments and illnesses in people who have disabilities compared to those without impairments (Mitra et al., 2009), some participants needed advanced treatment and drugs that were not available at public hospitals.

prioritised in terms of the allocation of the household economy rather than socioeconomic participation.

Personal assistance by caregivers

In most cases, it was expected that primary personal assistance for the disabled youth would be provided by family members, such as a parent, sibling, or relative. Caregivers' conditions were likely to be associated with socioeconomic participation, particularly when the disabled youth needed personal assistance to go outside. Some conditions, such as 'abandonment' of the disabled youth and 'health conditions of caregivers', were barriers to their current participation and would affect their future lifestyle, although the 'caregiver's views' might also have a relationship with the impacts.

Two participants had been abandoned by their parents due to their disabilities, indicating marginalisation and low-prioritisation of them within the household. A relative of one participant (no. 23) described the complicated household condition:

*She is a daughter of my dead husband's brother.
When she was a baby, her parents left her at this
house and disappeared somewhere. After that,
her nanny took care of her, but this nanny died
five years ago. Then, I'm just holding her in this
house....Because I also have to live in these poor
conditions, I cannot do extra things for her.
When the nanny was alive, she often took her to
a hospital and other places, but now I cannot do
so. Of course, I intend to hold her until I die*

because nobody takes care of her.

Another case (no. 12) whose divorced parents left her at a relative's house had a similar situation. These cases indicate that they did not have sufficient personal assistance for living and participation; these caregivers only provided necessities, such as bedding and minimal amounts of food, for these disabled youths.

The health condition of the caregivers was also an important factor associated with the socioeconomic participation of disabled youth. The most disastrous case in this study was a youth who had a psychiatric impairment but could communicate with others, including the research team members (no. 20). His mother's sister explained the situation:

When my husband was alive, he used to go outside with him. They sometimes went to a temple and his relative's houses....Now, his mother also has mental health problems, and assistance for him is insufficient. So we have no choice but keep him connected to the chain in his room almost all the time.

According to her, the reason to tether the youth to the chain was to prevent him from going somewhere and disappearing alone, which had happened before. This is the symbolic case of a conflict of interests between caregivers and the disabled person and extreme marginalisation at the household level. In other cases, the physical condition of the caregivers also affected the participation of the disabled youth, which was exemplified by one particular case of a participant (no. 6). Her caregiver, who was her mother, narrated her daughter's physical difficulties:

When she was a child, it was easier for me to hold her in my arm. But I have back pain now, and it is impossible to do so now [prams are not common in the area studied, so holding an infant or child in the caregiver's arm is common].

Hence, these illnesses of these caregivers were significant barriers to socioeconomic participation of the disabled youth.

The caregivers narrated their experiences and views, and they could be potential factors that influenced socioeconomic participation of the disabled youth. Some caregivers have emphasised the importance of their responsibility, even in difficult conditions. The mother of a youth (no. 5) expressed her view on her sense of responsibility as a parent, which could be a facilitator to the participation of the disabled youth:

I am struggling to live in the poor conditions of my household but trying to do as much as possible for my daughter. I know some parents who do not do anything for their disabled child, but I have a responsibility ('Wagakima'/ වගකීම) as a parent.

Perceived resource information and sociocultural image

The information and sociocultural image that caregivers had was related to the socioeconomic participation of the disabled youth. This theme included two subthemes: 'key persons and information' and 'sociocultural image'. Social services, ranging from vocational training centres and educational institutions to financial supports, were the fundamental resources for the promotion of the disabled youth's socioeconomic participation. From the perspective of the household level, availability was an important facilitator that impacted participation. In addition, the potential impact of a person's sociocultural image on disability was identified.

When the disabled youth considered participating in activities that certain organisations run, the information about these activities were essential facilitators ('key persons and information'). Key persons of the information included governmental officers, such as SSOs and 'Grama Niladhari' (village officers), and their personal network, such as other villagers. A mother of a youth who participated in a vocational training centre (no. 13) stated:

> *A social services officer visited our house to meet him through the Grama Niladhari's information. When he interviewed my son and us, the officer recommended he go to the training centre in Seeduwa.*

Some participants in this study went to SSOs directly. The mother of a person who had a physical impairment (no. 7) visited the office to meet the SSOs: 'They provided us information about all available vocational institutions for my son. We are discussing whether my son should utilise one of them'.

However, several participants did not have any information sources related to their participation. One of the typical answers was exemplified by a mother of a participant (no. 15):

I have never heard of such information. There is no place, isn't there? [Interviewer: For example, have you ever heard of this organisation?] No. I have not got such information....We have not met such an officer [SSO].

The narratives of caregivers implied that the issues of 'sociocultural image' also affected the socioeconomic participation of disabled youth. This potentially leads to a conflict of interests between caregivers and disabled persons. In the interviews in this study, two aspects were mentioned: the danger of going alone, and stigma.

Several caregivers, particularly parents, expressed concern about whether the disabled youth should travel somewhere and stay at an institution alone. These caregivers' concerns led to the limitation of participation and opportunities for going out. A description of a mother (no. 16) was an example of the concern that was also related to gender: 'Because she is female, we cannot allow her to go outside alone. It is too dangerous, and I have to take her anywhere'.

Another issue was the stigma of disability, which included shame and a perception of inability. Considering the following narrative of a mother of a young participant (no. 5), this is a potential barrier to the socioeconomic participation of the disabled youth: 'Some parents are ashamed ('Lajjayi'/ලැජ්ජයි) of taking them [the disabled youth] out because of their disability. So they tend to stay at home'. In addition, the views of inability were described by the mother of a person with an intellectual impairment: 'She cannot understand ('Teren-nae'/තේරෙන්

98

ஐ) or do anything because of her disability [However, she could speak a bit in front of the research team]'. Other stakeholders might have a prejudice against disabled people, which affects the household member's actions. The typical example was reported by the mother of a youth participant (no. 15): 'I asked Grama Niladhari about an ID card for her, but she said, "It is not necessary for her to make the ID card because she is a disabled"'.

4.3. Discussion

The association between conversion factors and socioeconomic participation

This situation analysis found an association between socioeconomic participation of the disabled youth and conversion and other factors at the household as well as individual levels. The findings of the quantitative survey and the qualitative study are integrated to allow the interpretation of the complicated contexts based on each research question.

First, in the quantitative survey, the overall extent of the achieved participation conditions was likely to be low amongst the study participants. Indeed, more than 65% of the participants answered 'not at all' or 'a little' for each component, except for 'culture/religion' (52.6%); the means of the sum of socioeconomic participation in all six components (2.1 ± 0.9) was close to the level of 'a little'. In addition, the number of participants who had educational experiences for less than two years (41.4%) appeared to be high. These findings support previous reports (Bieler, 2006; ESCAP, 1993; Mori et al., 2014) that showed limited participation opportunities of disabled people, although the measures were different.

The qualitative study explored the type of socioeconomic participation amongst disabled youth with a disadvantaged status. Those who had almost no opportunity for socioeconomic participation were identified ('almost nothing'), indicating the gap in the degree of socioeconomic participation between this type and other two types ('using institutions' and 'work in the community'). Nonetheless, most of them, even those who did not participate in the community regularly, reported taking part in religious activities outside the home.

Second, the quantitative survey identified the extent of the association of socioeconomic participation with conversion factors and some capability inputs. An analysis of this survey revealed a significant association of socioeconomic participation with the following factors: previous educational experiences, household monthly income and hardship, and connection with CBR. Therefore, a deprived status at the household and individual levels, such as inadequate schooling experiences, household hardship, and no connection with CBR, would be barriers to socioeconomic participation for disabled youth. A regression model with these conversion factors accounted for 41.3% of the variance of the socioeconomic participation variable. These findings were consistent with previous studies conducted in other countries (Barclay et al., 2016; Mori et al., 2014) that have shown the impacts of deprived conditions on the participation of disabled people.

In the qualitative study, four main themes that involved barriers and facilitators were generated based on the narratives of the disadvantaged participants. Consistent with the findings of the quantitative survey, previous educational and vocational experiences, household economic conditions, and perceived resource information were common themes, which could either be barriers or facilitators to socioeconomic participation depending upon the context. Personal assistance by caregivers and sociocultural images were also identified as having impacts on socioeconomic participation.

The qualitative study also indicated the complex dynamics within the household (Braithwaite & Mont, 2009), whereas the cross-sectional survey examined only the current conditions or a snapshot of the related factors. This observation supports findings of poverty dynamics, including 'survival struggles' (Grech, 2015: p.173), at the household level in developing countries. Indeed, the dynamics of socioeconomic participation and household conditions, including the marginalisation of the disabled youth under the prioritisation of household livelihood ('household economic conditions' and 'personal assistance by caregivers'), were complex at the lowest level.

Theoretical Implications

The findings provide the complicated implications for models of disability in terms of conversion factors at the household level. On one hand, the focus on the impacts of not only capability inputs but also conversion factors at the household level for disabled youth is significant because young people (and perhaps many disabled people) tend to be influenced by household conditions (Braithwaite & Mont, 2009; Filmer, 2008; WHO, 2007). As the findings of this research project show, socioeconomic participation of the disabled youth—freedom to participate, achieved participation, and choices—was likely to be affected by these household conditions, including household economic status and caregiver's health conditions, which were amongst the most important environmental factors.

On the other hand, a potential conflict of interest and the marginalisation of the disabled youth were observed between the participants. Many caregivers in the qualitative study expressed a struggle with their disadvantaged living and livelihood conditions. Caregivers and household members report burdensome experiences, which can be described as another type of 'disability' (Kuno, 2012; Kuno & Seddon, 2003) or 'disabled family' (Grech, 2015: p.104). However, as Kuno and Seddon (2003) argue, whilst the experiences of and burdens on the household members and caregivers are another important issue, this should not justify the restricted socioeconomic participation of disabled youth. Because the position of the disabled youth might be marginalised within the household, it is necessary to consider household conditions, including power-relationships, as conversion factors when discussing their socioeconomic participation. As a result, household conditions such as 'household economic conditions' and 'personal assistance by caregivers' in the findings of the qualitative study could still be placed with conversion factors, which could become either a barrier or a facilitator.

Previous Publication: This chapter is a revised and expanded version of my article: Higashida, M. (2017b). The relationship between the community participation of disabled youth and socioeconomic factors: Mixed-methods approach in rural Sri Lanka. *Disability & Society, 32*(8), pp.1239-1262.

CHAPTER FIVE

Situation Analysis in A Post-Conflict Environment

Conflict and war have long-term, devastating influences on public health across the globe (Ghobarah et al., 2004) and are associated with disability issues. Indeed, people have a high potential of becoming physically and psychosocially impaired due to war and conflict (Bogic et al., 2015; Summerfield, 2000; Thapa & Hauff, 2012). In addition, disability issues and voices of disabled people in conflict-affected areas are often marginalised from society (Eide, 2010; Moore, 2013; Rohwerder, 2013). Therefore, a situation analysis that sheds light on these issues and considers the sociocultural and post-conflict contexts as conversion factors are significant.

With respect to a post-conflict period at the grassroots level, evidence-based practical strategies and frameworks are indispensable to promoting the reconstruction of the affected society, which should involve disability issues (Eide, 2010; Kandasamy et al., 2016; Kett et al., 2005; WHO et al., 2010). CBR plays important roles in the realisation of the promotion of disabled people's socioeconomic participation. They are practical strategies that are implemented at the community level, including in armed conflict and emergency settings (Boyce, 2000; Eide, 2006, 2010; Peat, 1997; WHO et al., 2010). Revealing the impacts of and issues with CBR practice, together with a developmental social work perspective, is therefore necessary in a post-conflict environment. However, evidence and practical research on CBR in a post-conflict-affected area are quite likely limited in the global South (Eide, 2010; Kett et al., 2005). Hence, this situation analysis emphasises the importance of examining the impacts of developmental social work in CBR on socioeconomic participation of disabled people with a bottom-up research approach.

When planning and implementing developmental social work in CBR, sociocultural and political contexts are crucial because of their complexity and uniqueness in society. In other words, it is necessary to consider a context-specific perspective in a post-conflict area. I found the necessity of the situation analysis in the post-conflict environment of long-term civil war between the Sri Lankan government forces and the Liberation Tigers of Tamil Eelam (LTTE), which occurred from 1983 to 2009. Due to this war, many people experienced disabilities or were killed. According to the war-related casualty data from 1989 to 2009 (Uppsala Conflict Data Program, 2016), at least 65,372 people are estimated to have been killed during the civil war in Sri Lanka, particularly in the Northern and Eastern provinces where the LTTE had the control to claim an independent state for Tamil people. During and after the war, many stakeholders such as international institutions

(Siriwardhana et al., 2013) and non-government organisations (NGOs) provided aid in the provinces, including supportive programmes for disabled people (Kandasamy et al., 2016), although these stakeholders have complex political relationships and dilemmas (Goodhand & Lewer, 1999; Morais & Ahmad, 2011; Walton, 2008).

Although the literature reveals the health-related influences of and strategies against the civil war as well as the Indian Ocean earthquake and tsunami in 2004 in Sri Lanka, the evidence and study of CBR and developmental social work in the post-conflict era appears to be insufficient. The long-term impacts of the war, for instance, on the psychosocial well-being of the public (Keraite et al., 2016; Siriwardhana et al., 2015; Somasundaram, 2010), including people with forced displacement status (Husain et al, 2011; Siriwardhana & Wickramage, 2014), are reported. In addition, some international organisations, such as the WHO (Siriwardhana et al., 2013), and researchers (Taira et al., 2010) suggest programmes that strengthen the health-related professional resources in the Northern Province of Sri Lanka, whilst research underlines the importance of community resilience (Somasundaram & Sivayokan, 2013). Boyce (2000) has also discussed the potential positive impacts of CBR in conflict-affected areas during the civil war. Nevertheless, developmental social work in CBR in the post-conflict regions in Sri Lanka, as well as mental health promotion (Sritharan & Sritharan, 2014), seems to be missing from the mainstream literature. Hence, this study emphasises the necessity of practical research based on developmental social work in the CBR programme at the community level.

The objective of this situation analysis is to explore the situational context and the impacts of developmental social work in CBR on socioeconomic participation of disabled people in a post-conflict area of Sri Lanka. The research was implemented in October 2016, in collaboration with Vanni Rehabilitation Organisation for the Differently-Abled (VAROD), a local NGO, in the Mullaitivu district.

The VAROD is a non-religious oriented humanitarian organisation that was established by the Claretian Congregation of the Catholic Church (VAROD, 2016). The VAROD has conducted the CBR programme in the Mullaitivu district, which involves medical support, outreach services, physiotherapy, assistive devices, and livelihood supports, since 2011. A total 113 community rehabilitation committees (CRCs) hold regular meetings supported by five CBR workers of the VAROD—who are considered developmental social workers in this study—as of October 2016.

This situation analysis addresses the following research questions:

1. *What are the context and resultant issues facing disabled people in the post-conflict environment of Northern Sri Lanka?*

2. *What are the impacts of developmental social work in CBR on the socioeconomic participation of disabled people and their family members in the post-conflict environment?*

A mixed-methods approach was applied, including quantitative analysis of the NGO's registration database of disabled people in the area (n = 964), group interviews with nine CRCs of disabled people and their family members (n = 118), and semi-structured interviews with beneficiaries of the CBR programme (n = 5). Thematic analysis was applied to the narrative data.

5.1. Characteristics of Disabled People and Their Self-reported Needs

From the quantitative data analysis, Table 11 shows the characteristics of 964 disabled people from the VAROD database as of October 2016. The average age was 32.5 years old: 33.4 years old for males and 31.2 years old for females. The percentage of disabled men (59.8%) was larger than that of disabled women (40.2%). Physical impairments, including vision, hearing, and speech, were the most common impairments (83.6%), whereas intellectual and/or developmental impairments, psychiatric impairments, and multiple impairments were less common (5.7%, 3.0%, and 3.9% respectively). Regarding the relationship with conflict, the proportion of war-related impairments was 60.9%, followed by birth-related impairments (21.0%), and disease-related impairments (7.6%) such as communicable diseases. Most war-related impairments were caused by shelling and air-attacks, mines, and gunshots.[25]

---

[25] Because of the insufficient information on the database, the proportion was not calculated.

Table 11: Type and cause of impairment identified by the VAROD in the Mullaitivu district

	Male (n=576)		Female (n=388)		Total (n=964)	
Average age (years)	33.4		31.2		32.5	
Type of impairment						
Physical	500	86.8%	306	78.9%	806	83.6%
(Speech and/or hearing)	(43)		(32)		(75)	
(Visual)	(37)		(22)		(59)	
Neurological and/or epilepsy	13	2.3%	19	4.9%	32	3.3%
Intellectual and/or Developmental	27	4.7%	28	7.2%	55	5.7%
Psychiatric	13	2.3%	16	4.1%	29	3.0%
Multiple	22	3.8%	16	4.1%	38	3.9%
Other or unclear	1	0.2%	3	0.8%	4	0.4%
Cause of impairment						
War-related event	362	62.8%	225	58.0%	587	60.9%
Birth	112	19.4%	90	23.2%	202	21.0%
Disease	39	6.8%	34	8.8%	73	7.6%
Accident	25	4.3%	18	4.6%	43	4.5%
Tsunami in 2004	2	0.3%	0	0.0%	2	0.2%
Other or unclear	36	6.3%	21	5.4%	57	5.9%

Note: Adapted from Higashida, Soosai, & Robert (2017).

Of 964 disabled people, the self-reported needs of 194 beneficiaries were available for analysis (Table 12). Livelihood assistance (44.6%) was the most common type of need amongst disabled people, followed by medical supports (15.3%) and assistive devices (11.9%). The expressed needs of livelihood assistance included employment opportunities and support for micro self-employment using microcredit loans.

5.2. Impacts of Community Rehabilitation Committees and Social Investment in the Post-Conflict Area

A crucial resource

Due to limited local resources in each studied area of the Mullaitivu district, CRCs and the livelihood assistance programme—which were supported by CBR workers—were crucial resources for these participants (Figure 9). There are some local resources for the public in each village. For instance, a female participant (CRC-3) who is a family member of a disabled person stated, 'There are two types of women's committees in my village. The one is a general committee for women aged over 18 years old, and the other is a supportive committee for domestic violence and so on'. In addition, local government offices provide some supports for disabled people, such as social welfare allowance (Rs. 3,000), but the range of beneficiaries and impacts are likely inadequate. Many participants at the group interviews reported a shortage of local resources for disabled people. A disabled male (CRC-3) explained, 'Some of the participants in this CRC receive supports, like Rs. 3,000 monthly and home renovation subsidy, through the AG [administrative government] office, but that's all—neither more nor less'. As the following narrative shows, many participants from the group interviews described CRCs as a sole active resource: 'There is no resource for disabled people in this area except for this group [CRC]' (Disabled male, CRC-6).

Table 12: Self-reported need identified by the VAROD in the Mullaitivu district

Rank	Need	Number	%	Example
1	Livelihood assistance	90	44.6%	Job, manufacturing equipment, livelihood loan
2	Medical aids	31	15.3%	Treatment, detailed examination, medical bills
3	Assistive devices	24	11.9%	Wheel-chair, hearing aid
4	Education	23	11.4%	Education, training
5	Rehabilitation	13	6.4%	Physiotherapy, psychosocial rehabilitation
6	Nutrition	11	5.4%	Nutritious foods
7	Accommodation /house	10	5.0%	House, repairing, water pump
	Total	202	100.0%	

Note: Adapted from Higashida, Soosai, & Robert (2017). Multiple responses were allowed during the data collection by CBR workers.

Self-help and psychosocial support

Various positive functions of CRCs, including self-help and mutual support within a group, were observed in some CRCs. The leader of a committee (CRC-2), who is a disabled male, stressed the necessity of empowering the group: 'Although this CRC was established by the support of the VAROD, we should solve the daily issues by ourselves within this CRC. We need to further develop this CRC by ourselves'. A disabled female (CRC-3) described a positive aspect of the committee as follows: 'We can share and put together our needs as a group. The needs would include livelihood assistance, medical supports, and assistive devices and so forth'. Another disabled male (CRC-9), who has a physical impairment, put it this way: 'For example, some of us [in this CRC] visit other disabled people's houses regularly. When I identified the needs of the disabled person, I supported him to submit an application to an organisation'. In the group interviews (CRC-9), five participants stated regular voluntary visits to other disabled people's houses.

Figure 9. Community rehabilitation committee (CRC)

Note: I obtained the participants' permission to take and use this photo in 2016.

Governance by disabled people of CRCs

Participants of some CRCs emphasised the importance of developing their livelihood conditions as an agency. According to them, they have the capability of handling the loan system whilst revolving it properly; as a result, CRC members can gain benefits through the programme. A disabled male (CRC-6) explained the importance of the livelihood assistance: 'Actually, there are extremely few employment opportunities for disabled people, particularly long-term or permanent contract. So livelihood is very important for us. Whilst revolving the loan, we can manage it as a group, share the benefits, and develop it by ourselves'. Another disabled male (CRC-8) also stated: 'Because this area is wide, available resources are scattered, and, actually, scarce. So, if we can start something like "Kadai" [retail store], we can improve and develop our livelihood'.

Improved socioeconomic participation

Indeed, interview data analysis found positive impacts of developmental social activities on livelihood and income conditions at the household level. Most of the beneficiaries of the livelihood assistance programme who were interviewed stated improved economic conditions that would have positive impacts on the quality of life of their family members. The types of assisted livelihoods included poultry, livestock breeding, sewing, retail shop, agriculture, and others. A female (CRC-5) who has a physical impairment due to shelling and whose husband was killed during the civil war said, 'Using the loan [of the livelihood assistance programme], I bought a sewing machine two years ago. I sew clothes and bags for selling. I earn about Rs. 300 to 500 daily. Because my husband died, this is a very important income source for my family. Thanks to the assistance, my son can receive education at school'. In addition, a wife of a disabled male (CRC-1) explained that they started a poultry business using a microcredit loan, and that they have already repaid the loan: 'We have about 40 chickens. For example, on a day that they lay 15 eggs, we can earn Rs. 225....Because my husband has a physical impairment due to the war, this is basically our sole income source. Although my brothers sometimes visit to support, the chickens are an important income source for us'.

5.3. Issues with developmental social work in CBR in a Post-Conflict Area

Limited participation

By contrast, some potentially negative aspects of developmental social activities were observed. Active participants in CRCs, for instance, appeared to be fixed; some disabled people would not attend CRCs. Several possible reasons were mentioned by participants. A disabled female (CRC-5) stated the following potential reasons: 'I think members, who have a job or have to take care of their family members like disabled people and children, have difficulties attending the CRC. Those who can manage it are able to participate in it'. Another case (HV-1) was exemplified by the father of a disabled boy: 'Honestly, I just sometimes join it [the CRC]. If we go to take him [disabled son], we need two carers because of his physical impairment and problem of moving. I work at a school every day, and it's difficult to manage time and assistances to attend the committee'.

Demotivation and expectations of financial aid

The most common issue, however, was the demotivation of CRC members to attend due to the perceived lack of financial benefits; some ex-participants stopped attending CRCs after they noticed that they could not receive a livelihood assistance loan immediately. The typical narrative was stated by the leader of a CRC who is a disabled male

(CRC-8): 'Some of them just stopped to attend this CRC because they perceived no financial and immediate benefits through the committee'. According to another disabled male (CRC-5): 'In this CRC, 28 members are registered, but only six members regularly participate in meetings. The main reason is like, if they notice there is no financial aid, they don't come to the next meeting'. This implies that some members recognised CRCs solely as a medium of livelihood assistance, or a loan, which might create a gap between supported and unsupported beneficiaries of the livelihood assistance. Thus, some participants may only depend on, or expect, the livelihood assistance programme or direct financial merits, which lead to demotivation of attendance, instead of self-help and empowerment by disabled people themselves.

Marginalisation of some disabled people in CBR

In addition, most participants of CRCs had war-related impairments. In the CRC-9, for instance, people who have war-related impairments are registered, although the regulations of CRCs involve those who have any type of impairment. A disabled male (CRC-4) stated, 'Actually, we know people with intellectual and psychosocial impairments in this village. We have contacted them, but they have not attended this CRC....There may be several reasons, like old age and employed conditions of the family members....Well, some of the family members would not want to take them outside because of shame or something'. This implies that participations of those who have intellectual and psychiatric impairments unrelated to the war have perhaps not been promoted in some CRCs.

Competition between stakeholders

Another issue is the relationship between organisations from the perspective of disabled people and their family members. Some participants expressed concerns about the competition between actors. A disabled male (CRC-9) expressed the following issue: 'We want to help each other, but sometimes the competition between organisations hinder our activities. After the end of the conflict, many organisations came to this area....As a result, we were tossed by the political relationship'. He continued to explain the details, such as an organisation's unnecessary aid programme that was already provided by another organisation.

5.4. Discussion

This situation analysis attempted to explore the situational context and the impacts of developmental social activities in an NGO's CBR programme on socioeconomic participation of disabled people in the post-conflict areas of Sri Lanka. The findings of the quantitative and qualitative analysis make several important observations regarding the potential impacts of developmental social work in CBR in the field of post-conflict and disability. I discuss the following issues based on these findings: reflection on the relationship amongst post-conflict, disability, and CBR, and the potential issues with developmental social work in CBR in the post-conflict period. The discussion points out the importance of a sustainable approach and capacity building, whilst also shedding light on the potential marginalisation in disability issues.

Conversions factors related to the post-conflict environment

The impacts of the war were observed by quantitative and qualitative data analysis, whilst revealing the significance of developmental social work in CBR in the post-conflict environment, which is consistent with arguments of the literature (Boyce, 2000; Eide,

2010; WHO et al., 2010). Although this is not a population epidemiological survey, 60.9% of beneficiaries of the CBR programme have war-related impairments in the Mullaitivu district. This implies the long-term influences of war-related health conditions and other conversion factors in the affected areas seven years after the end of the civil war.

In addition to the health conditions, livelihood and economic conditions such as poverty and hardship (Korf, 2004) still appeared to be amongst the most important issues for disabled people in the sites studied by quantitative and qualitative analysis. The CBR programme that consists of CRCs and livelihood assistance, or a social investment intervention strategy (Midgley & Conley, 2010), was likely to correspond to their needs and have positive impacts on their life.

Challenges with expectations and marginalisation

I observed some controversial issues with developmental social work in CBR in the post-conflict region through this case study of an NGO programme. The potential issues included the gap in expectations between beneficiaries and marginalised people. I argue that these issues could happen in each post-conflict field; therefore, it is important to consider the promotion of sustainable development for DPOs and the empowerment of them.

First, the expectation of 'beneficiaries' of the financial assistance by an organisation—which could be capability inputs—is controversial. It is necessary to provide various forms of assistance, including financial aid, to conflict-affected disabled people through programmes of multiple organisations (Inter-agency working group on reproductive health in crises, 2010; WHO et al., 2010). The relationship between livelihood assistance and self-help nature would not necessarily be contradicted.

116

Although quantitative and qualitative analysis also identified the necessity of livelihood assistance, which supports the arguments in the literature (Korf, 2004), financial assistance might include negative aspects. In the case of CRCs that rely on the microcredit loan programme of an organisation, participants would become interested in the budget management and financial benefits, instead of self-help and community mobilisation. Indeed, some members seem to be demotivated to attend a CRC because of a perceived lack of financial benefits, although it was apparently their choice. Hence, strategies for the sustainable development and empowerment, such as a shift in position from beneficiaries/recipients to citizens, experts, activists, and an agency of change (Davidson, 2005; Mathie & Cunningham, 2003; Rifkin & Kangare, 2002) and the capacity building of DPOs, are necessary to be considered in developmental social work during and after conflict.

Second, potentially marginalised disabled people were identified in the sites studied. As Rohwerder (2013) indicates, people with certain types of impairment may be further marginalised in the sociocultural context—this is also considered a conversion factor. In this situation analysis, most research participants appeared to be disabled people who have war-related physical impairments. As some of the participants mentioned, some committees would not promote involving people with certain kinds of impairments, such as intellectual, developmental, and psychiatric impairments, though they did not intend to exclude them. I then argue that the active involvement of disabled people that are not related to the war is also important for promoting participation in developmental social work.

Previous Publication: This chapter is a revised and expanded version of Higashida, M., Soosai, J., & Robert, J. (2017). The impact of community-based rehabilitation in a post-conflict environment of Sri Lanka. *Disability, CBR & Inclusive Development, 28*(1), pp.93-111.

CHAPTER SIX

Situation Analysis In A Model Area Of CBR

Since Richmond (1922), an American social work pioneer, spoke of the importance of actions in social work in many parts of the social environment and issues, 'local resources' or 'social resources'[26] have been recognised as one of the key factors in social work practices. As discussed in Chapter 1 from the perspective of developmental social work with the capability approach, resources can be converted into the foundation for a person's capability set and opportunities for

---

[26] In this paper, they are described as local resource(s), although this term is not standardised. In addition, the concept of local resources has a mutually complimentary relation to the theory of 'social capital', which emphasises the relationships and norms in society.

socioeconomic participation. In this situation analysis, the concept of 'resources' is defined as 'any existing service or commodity that can be called on to help take care of a need…[including] other social agencies, government programs, other professional or volunteer personnel, self-help groups, natural helpers, and individuals in the community' (Barker, 1999: p. 412).

The structure of local resources in CBR is unequally mentioned amongst researchers. For instance, Peat (1997) describes three factors that support CBR from both the internal and external perspectives of a local community: human resources, structural resources, and attitudes. Finkenflügel et al. (2005) note, in their review of evaluative articles on CBR, the concept of local resources such as the use of local technologies and their cost effectiveness as important elements in enabling the sustainability of CBR programmes. Mitchell (1999) also supports the notion that local resources and referral systems are key factors in CBR. The classification of four types of resources in CBR is presented in Table 13. This situation analysis mainly focuses on human resources and structural resources inside a community, which are the most important factors for any community development programme (Peat, 1997).

Table 13: Types and examples of resources in CBR

Types of Resource	Inside a Community	Outside a Community
Human Resource	Disabled people, their family members (caregivers), CBR volunteers/workers, local officers	Health and welfare professionals, strategic planners, international volunteers
Structural Resource	Existing community groups and agencies, local government offices, religious institutions	Central government ministries, NGOs/INGOs
Institutional Resource	Locally agreed-upon rules, local services systems	National policy, Convention on the Rights of Persons with Disabilities
Financial Resource	Local joint funds (own funds), local government budgets	National budget, international funds

Note: Adapted from Higashida (2014b). Summarised from Peat (1997) and Finkenflügel et al.(2005), whilst adding examples and 'institutional resources'.

Although CBR has been studied by various researchers and practitioners, including evaluative research at the grassroots level (Biggeri et al., 2014), studies on the relationship between socioeconomic participation and local resources is noticeably limited (Finkenflügel et al., 2005). With the overall purpose of identifying the distinctive features of the CBR model area in Sri Lanka, the objective of this situation analysis is to examine the socioeconomic participation of disabled people who utilise local resources.

This study used data from semi-structured interviews with disabled people (n = 18)—including 11 users and 7 non-users of local resources—, interviews with an SSO, documents relevant to CBR, and the author's field notes in the R-division. Thematic analysis was applied to the narrative data.

6.1. Overall Assessment of Local Resources

The number of disabled people registered by the DS was 363 as of December 2012. The proportion of disabled people in the R-division was approximately 1.1% of 32,684 residents in 2012.[27] Because there was no accurate information on disabled people in the local government office, I organised the information on the basis of the type of impairments, which was collected by Japan Overseas Cooperation Volunteers (JOCVs) in 2009 (Table 14). The average age was 39.9 years old. The percentage of disabled men (58.4%) was larger than that of disabled women (41.6%). Physical impairments were reported by a majority (68.2%), whilst psychiatric or neurological impairments including epilepsy garnered 5.9%.

According to data from the interview with the SSO, the local resources available to disabled people were extremely limited in 2008. Since the present SSO was assigned in 2008, disabled people, their families, the SSO, and JOCVs have developed local resources and social investment activities such as community workshops and CBR village steering committees.

Figure 10 shows a schematic diagram of the stakeholders and local resources in the CBR programme in the R-division in 2013, which was updated in 2017. Two SSOs worked for elderly people, disabled people, and single-parent families at the local government office in the

---

[27] According to the World Bank and the WHO (2011), 2.9% is the proportion of persons with severe disabilities in the world whist 15.3% is said to be the average of disabled people in the world. This implies that there are certain numbers of potential/hidden disabled people who are not reflected in statistics although it may not be appropriate to compare two different types of percentages under the same condition.

R-division. However, there was only one officer mainly in charge of disability issues. The SSO takes charge of wide-ranging developmental social work activities, including management and coordination of programmes. It is obvious that a single SSO cannot comprehensively perform all the duties with respect to social services in the vast local administrative division.

Table 14: Type of impairment identified in the R-division

Types of impairment	Total	% of Total	Male	% of Male	Female	% of Female	Average age
Physical	220	68.8	132	60.0	88	40.0	45.8
(Visual, hearing, and/or speaking)	(74)	-	(44)	(59.5)	(30)	(40.5)	(40.8)
(Mobility)	(155)	-	(93)	(60.0)	(62)	(40.0)	(48.4)
Intellectual	58	18.1	32	55.2	26	44.8	24.5
Psychiatric*	19	5.9	10	52.6	9	47.4	38.2
Multiple	18	5.6	9	50.0	9	50.0	25.4
Other or unclear	5	1.6	4	80.0	1	20.0	24.2
Total	320	100.0	187	58.4	133	41.6	39.9

Notes: Revised version of Higashida's (2014b) table. * Includes epilepsy.

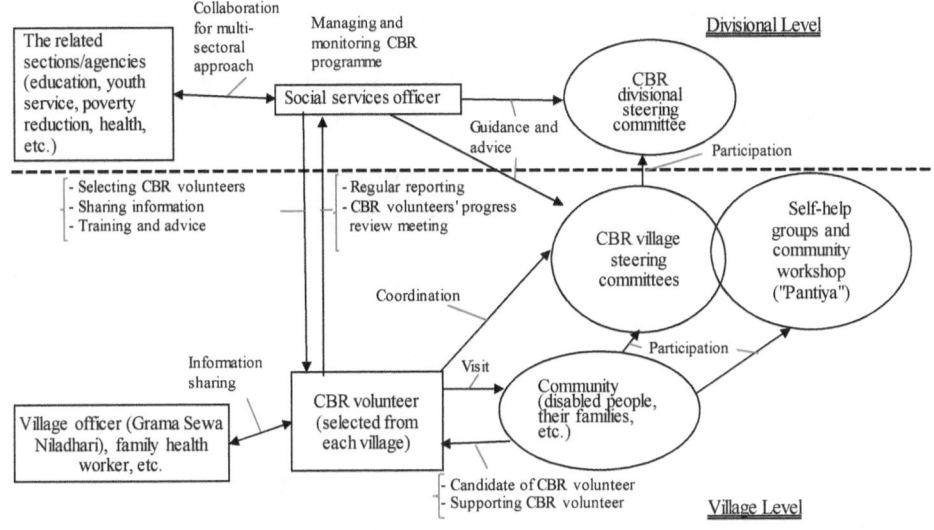

Figure 10. Relation diagram of CBR stakeholders and main local resources in the R-division

Note: Revised version of Higashida's (2014b) figure.

CBR volunteers were expected to enrol newly disabled people, provide necessary personal support for disabled people, offer advice and guidance to caregivers, and hold village steering committees in order to compensate for the shortage of professionals and local government officers. The number of CBR volunteers registered by the local government office was about 17, including a few disabled people, as of April 2013. However, the number of disabled people and their families who received supports from CBR volunteers was limited.

Under the facilitation of the SSO, self-help groups were held once monthly. CBR village steering committees were also held continually in five villages, once every two months, and community workshops were run in two villages in the R-division.

In terms of education, eleven disabled children received inclusive

123

education in the Montessori preschools in 2013. A total of 19 disabled pupils were registered in the two special needs education classes. In addition, through collaborative practices of the SSO and the youth services officer (YSO), disabled people participated in youth club events such as a youth camp and a sports festival on a regular basis.

6.2. Community Workshop, 'Pantiya'

The community workshops ('Pantiya'/පංතිය, 'Puhunu Pantiya'/පුහුණු පංතිය or 'Ape Iskolaya'/අපේ ඉස්කෝලය) were developed as a unique social investment activity in Anuradhapura district, one of which started in 2009 (Figure 11). 'Pantiya' was held weekly at a temple or participants' houses. Seven disabled people regularly participated in 'Pantiya' in the initial phase. Activities were developed by the SSO and CBR volunteers, based on field visits in training centres in other districts. The contents of the activities (e.g., occupational activities) were mainly proposed by the members of 'Pantiya'. In addition, participants sold products around their houses and in the shop of 'Pantiya' in order to collect operating funds.

As of 2017, two 'Panitya' were operated in the R-division: one was held once or twice a week at a vacant land of a government office, and the other was held weekly at a temple. The main contents of the activity were the manufacturing of daily necessaries, which were mainly conceived of by families and the SSO. Totally around 30 members participated regularly in two 'Pantiya'. The participants also held regular meetings and markets.

Figure 11. 'Pantiya' in the R-division

Note: I obtained the participants' permission to take and use these photos in 2013.

6.3. Socioeconomic Participation of Disabled People Who Utilise Local Resources

Figure 12 was created based on the analysis of semi-structured interviews aimed at clarifying life histories relating to the use of local resources. The results revealed individual level elements at each stage: infancy, school age, after school age, turning points, and after participation.

Significant factors are pointed out as shown below. First, 'meeting with a key person', such as the SSO and other supporters in the community, was one of the 'turning points' in the lives of the users of 'Pantiya'. Even nine users of 'Pantiya' did not meet the SSO or receive any support from the previous SSOs for more than one year after school age before 2009. The average period during which the users of 'Pantiya' had been isolated from the community after school age ('social withdrawal') was approximately 7.7 years. Taken together with the ratio of disabled people in the R-division, it implied that many disabled people had no direct links to local resources.

Second, 'Pantiya' included a variety of functions as one of the local resources in the R-division ('improving quality of life'). For example, disabled people developed manufacturing techniques and increased their income by selling products at the weekly market. Respectively, five and nine users of 'Pantiya' stated that their income had increased and that they manufactured products at home. Interviewee no. 3 said, 'I am satisfied with my life. If there isn't our "Pantiya", I have to spend all the time in my house....I can be skilled in manufacturing activities here'. In addition, all users of 'Pantiya' reported that they had opportunities to build social support networks with others, and seven users joined the meetings and events in the R-division, such as youth clubs and funeral unions. Interviewee no.1 stated, 'Now, I can go to various places! And,

126

I've got a lot of friends'.

Furthermore, two interviewees worked as CBR volunteers ('candidate of CBR volunteer') and one interviewee became a salesperson at a shop ('job') after started participating in 'Pantiya'. For instance, interviewee no. 5 said, 'I needed somebody's assistance and help in the past, but…now it is possible for me to help someone, because I have participated in CBR for many years. If my disabled friends face difficulties that are similar to my experience, I may be able to support them. Because I have the knowledge to do so'.

The analysis also indicates that the division's CBR programme encountered challenges relating to disabled people's rights to receive education, information sharing and networking, and the availability of local resources, amongst others. First, those who dropped out (eight interviewees in 'dropout') and were out-of-school (one interviewee in 'out-of-school') were identified even amongst users of 'Pantiya'. Reasons for 'dropout' were not only attributed to personal factors but also environmental factors, including the 'closure of classroom' for disabled pupils. Similar challenges were revealed in a research by a local NGO (AKASA, 2011).

Second, four users of 'Pantiya' (nos. 7, 9, 11 and 13) and all non-users mentioned the lack of a network and of information. After their schooling period, even users of 'Pantiya' and their families had almost no connection with SSOs and other frontline officers or other disabled people. In four cases, not only disabled people but also their family members did not recognise the CBR activities and related stakeholders.

Third, four users of 'Pantiya' (nos. 8, 9, 11 and 13) and all non-users stated indifference or rejection of resource usages. For instance, interviewee no. 13 simply said, 'I don't want to go there'. His mother explained that he was not used to interacting with others because he stopped going to school within 6 months owing to learning difficulties and a lack of educational supports in the regular class. In the case of this interviewee, unwillingness to go to school is possibly due to the short period of education and negative experiences during education: indeed, it is worth noting that only the four families of non-users of 'Pantiya' (nos. 6, 7, 9 and 11) mentioned negative experiences during the schooling period ('problem'), as compared with users of 'Pantiya' (nos. 1–5).

Family priorities might also be related to reasons for a disabled person's unwillingness to participate in socioeconomic activities. For example, interviewee no. 7 said, 'I do daily chores every day and play with my cousin'. The parent said that it was helpful and keeping them at home required little effort. His mother's narratives and household contexts, including apparent hardship, indicated that they did not want to change their household lifestyle.

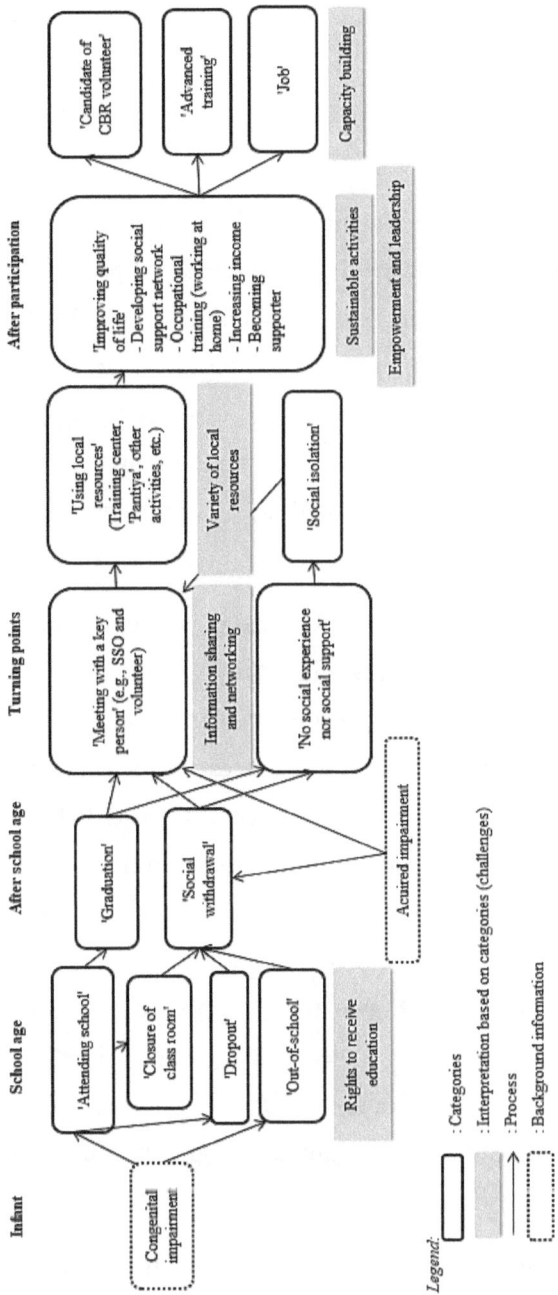

Figure 12: Analysis diagram of the life history in relation to local resources

Note: Adapted from Higashida (2014b).

6.4. Discussion

Summary

The findings of this situation analysis suggest that compared to 2008, when local resource availability to disabled people was extremely limited, the social participation opportunities of disabled people have improved through the development of local resources since 2009. In particular, using existent resources (e.g., manufacturing techniques and available places), disabled people, their families, and the SSO developed 'Pantiya', which can be regarded as an important model of local resources.

The focal point, however, for challenges in the R-division is as follows: whilst participants in the 'Pantiya' improved their socioeconomic participation to a certain extent, a limited number of other disabled people were introduced to the occasion. The number of disabled people registered by the local government office was 363, and only about 10% of this figure participates in 'Pantiya'. Even though disabled people in some divisions in Anuradhapura district were willing to participate in local resources, the resource levels might be insufficient to match their needs, or it might not be available because of poor or non-existent accessibility conditions. In other words, some disabled people had extremely limited range of potential functionings—restricted freedom to participate—due to the poor resource setting. The following challenges are therefore implied from these findings.

First, according to reported needs of the participants through dialogue, it is necessary to develop more resources, such as 'Pantiya', in the R-division as well as in other divisions, using existing local resources.

It is also essential that disabled people and their families take initiatives to proactively develop local resources as a process of empowerment. Second, building networks amongst stakeholders is also required for the sake of those who are not connected to local resources including 'Pantiya' and schools. For instance, it is indispensable for CBR volunteers to undertake active outreach to disabled people isolated from the society under the facilitation of SSOs.

Practical Implications

This chapter focused on the development and utilisation of locally available resources in the community. The concept of local resources in CBR is large in scope and can range from human resources (WHO et al., 2010) to appropriate technologies and financial aspects (Peat, 1997). This situation analysis examined multiple aspects of local resources, such as processes of development, interrelationships amongst human resources (e.g., disabled people, their families and SSOs) and structural resources (e.g., 'Pantiya', temples and schools), as well as the impacts on the freedom to participate and achieved socioeconomic participation of disabled people. Additionally, these factors were analysed at the individual level and the community level, and it would be possible to also explore them at the group and meso-level.

One of the reasons for the concept of local resources having such a wide range of aspects is because it is practice-oriented. As a practical matter, the concept is useful for developmental social work practitioners to conduct CBR programmes for further community development as well as personal assistance. From the developmental social work perspective, local people may be able to comprehensively recognise and share local conditions and to create synergy amongst existing local resources in

131

community development through collaborative practices. In other words, from the view point of the capability approach, this case study also highlighted the possibilities and values of local resource development for expanding disabled people's capability set.

Previous Publication: This chapter is a revised and updated version of my article: Higashida, M. (2014). Local resources of disabled people in Sri Lanka: Action research on community-based rehabilitation programme. *Sociology and Anthropology, 2*(4), 159-167.

CHAPTER SEVEN

Practice 1: Developing Local Resources

Developing local resources as social investment is an important strategy in developmental social work. As indicated in Section 1.3, it could contribute to the expansion of disabled people's capability set, or freedom to participate, perhaps followed by having choices and achieving functionings. The objective of this follow-up study of Chapter 6 is to examine the factors of developing local resources as a developmental social work practice in the CBR programme in the Anuradhapura district, including the R-division. Of all the resources, the study mainly focuses on community workshops[28].

---

[28] There were also nine vocational training centres for disabled people in Sri Lanka as of 2017. Although no centre has been established in the Anuradhapura district, selected

The target study site was the Anuradhapura district, which consists of 22 government administrative divisions including the R-division, AI-division, AT1-division, AT2-division, AM-division and AP-division. In the Anuradhapura district, self-help groups are held once a month in each division.

The community workshops ('Pantiya'; See also Chapter 6) were developed as a unique group activity in the Anuradhapura district, one of which started in the R-division in 2009. The objective is to empower disabled youth and children as well as to increase their income, although this has not been officially documented. Regular activities include the manufacturing of daily necessities and social activities. The participants of some community workshops also hold markets to sell their products.

7.1. Strategy and Process

Using the results of research (Chapter 6), stakeholders of the CBR programme including the SSO in the R-division and I planned to develop community workshops in the Anuradhapura district in line with dialogue with the chief SSO; we also recommended launching community workshops in each division in reference to the model practice of the R-division. We decided to promote the launch of community workshops with disabled people and their family members in the district, towards the development of local resources to empower disabled people and improve their quality of life.

As shown in Table 15, whilst setting five pilot divisions (R-division,

disabled youth can participate in training. One of the most striking features of the district is that no non-government organisation (NGO) has directly implemented a CBR programme, although some local NGOs, such as AKASA (2011) have conducted programmes on disability issues.

AI-division, AM-division, AT1-division, and AT2-division) in the district, the participants of community workshops in the R-division, including disabled people, their family members, SSOs, and myself, conducted outreach courses in the divisions. Whilst the contents of the activities were based on the R-division's practice through the outreach course, regular activities—such as the manufacture of daily necessities—and operational methods were determined by participants at each community workshop: disabled people, their families, and SSOs. The members of community workshops were required to bring raw materials or raise funds to procure materials and equipment by selling products and vegetables, or by collecting a small amount of money at the beginning of the project. As a result, the new community workshops were launched in six divisions including the non-target area (AP-division).

Disabled people and SSOs in AM-division, AI-division, AT1-division, and AT2-division visited the R-division more than once during the study period, in order to learn how to run community workshops. Progress was shared with SSOs in monthly meetings.

Regarding the data collection and analysis, the study used narrative data from semi-structured interviews with the participants (disabled people) of community workshops (n = 24), separate focus group discussion with the participants (n = 34), and the SSOs (n = 5), and the author's field notes. Data were analysed within the framework of strengths, weaknesses, opportunities, and threats (Box 6).

Table 15: Target divisions promoting the community workshop

Site	Opening year	Continuity	Frequency	Place	Outreach courses
R-1	2009	Yes	1-2/w	Government building	-
R-2	Jul 2013	Yes	1/w	Temple	3 times
AI-1	2012	Yes	1/w	Government building	-
AI-2	Feb 2014	Yes	1-2/m	Community centre	2 times
AT1	Sep 2013	Yes	1/w	Samrudhi* meeting room	3 times
AM	Sep 2013	Yes	1-2/m	Vidhata** room	5 times
AT2	Jul 2013	No	1/m	Divisional Secretariat	5 times
AP	Apr 2014	Yes	1/w	Montessori	-

Note: Adapted from Higashida, Illangasingha, & Kumara (2015).
* Section of poverty reduction; ** Branch of the Ministry of Technology and Research

Box 6: SWOT Analysis in This Study

The framework of strengths, weaknesses, opportunities, and threats (SWOT) analysis was used to analyse narrative data. Sharma and Deepak (2001) also used this method to evaluate the CBR programme in Vietnam. The characteristics of SWOT were clarified with reference to Kuipers et al. (2003) as follows.

	Positive	Negative
Internal	**Strengths:** Positive characteristics that were internal to local resources and could support future development, and advantages of the resources.	**Weaknesses:** Negative internal characteristics and the disadvantages of local resources.
External	**Opportunities:** Positive characteristics and favourable trends that were external to local resources and could be harnessed.	**Threats:** Negative characteristics that were external to local resources and acted as obstacles, competing demands or forces that could cause damage in the future.

Source: Higashida, Illangasingha & Kumara (2015).

7.2. Strengths, Weaknesses, Opportunities, and Threats

As shown in Table 16, the results are drawn from the narrative data of participants in community workshops and local government officers separately, in line with the framework of strengths, weaknesses, opportunities, and threats. Although each community workshop has different situations, the content of the narrative data was generally similar, except for the R-division, which had the initiative to develop community workshops in the Anuradhapura district. The following results are therefore integrated.

Strengths

Five elements of strengths were identified from data in the narratives of the participants and SSOs. 'Increase of income' was noted by both groups. This element corresponds to the purpose of holding community workshops. A female interviewee in the R-1 (52 years old, physical impairment) said:

Table 16: SWOT Matrix by participants of community workshops and social services officers

SWOT	Participants	Social Services Officers
Strengths	- Increase of income - Capacity development - Making friends - Sense of unity and equality - Operation by discussion	- Increase of income - Capacity development - Expansion of future opportunities - Unity amongst disabled people and their families - Awareness-raising
Weaknesses	- Gap of degrees in impairments and capacities - Instability of the venue - Difficulty in procurement of tools and equipment - Lack of operating funds	- Decrease and immobilisation of the participants - Too much time before results is realised - Difficulty in procurement of tools and equipment
Opportunities	- Presence of model activities - Opportunities for interaction and mutual support - Existing techniques	- Accumulated past experiences within the district - Existing resources and collaborators - Evaluation of the matter at a national level - Possibility of funding from the central government
Threats	- Poor transport links and accessibility	- Poor transport links and accessibility - Lack of understanding by families - Secondary effects of disability benefits - Instability of support by the officers

Note: Adapted from Higashida, Illangasingha, & Kumara (2015).

I walk around the village to sell products which I manufacture in 'Pantiya'. I also sell products made in my house using techniques learnt in

139

'Pantiya'. Since coming to 'Pantiya', my daily
income has increased. So, I'm happy.

A male interviewee in the AM-division (45 years old, physical impairment) also stated:

Because I learnt how to make a 'Papissa'
(පාපිස්ස, doormat in Sinhalese) and other
products here, now I can wholesale such
products. I can make a 'Papissa' in two to three
days. It is possible for me to sell them in Rs. 150.

The SSO in the R-division said during a focus group discussion, 'I believe that the goal of holding community workshops is to increase the income of disabled people and their families'.

'Capacity development' was also described by disabled people and SSOs. A male interviewee in the AM-division (30 years old, multiple impairments) said, 'I don't like to waste time in my house without any activities. I feel pleasure when I come to "Pantiya" because I can develop my skills to manufacture products. I want to do something rather than be helped by someone'. The SSO noted that participants can develop not only manufacturing techniques but also social skills through socialising with other participants, which can lead to 'expansion of future opportunities' such as religious events, compulsory education, advanced training centres, and self-employed jobs. In addition, 'making friends' is important for participants. A female interviewee in the R-1 (36, psychiatric impairment) said, 'It is enjoyable for me to meet peers and

140

learn how to make products. Before I came here, I didn't have these opportunities'.

In terms of positive group dynamics, participants noted a 'sense of unity and equality'. A male interviewee in the AM-division (75, physical impairment) said, 'Everyone seems to be in the same position here'. An interviewee in the R-1 (26, physical impairment) described the strengths as 'cooperation and unity of all'. SSOs also recognised 'unity amongst disabled people and their families'.

Participants noted 'operation by discussion' as the strength of community workshops, which enhanced the unity. A female interviewee in the R-1 (19, intellectual impairment) said, 'We discuss things together in meetings to solve issues or plan new activities'.

SSOs mentioned 'awareness-raising' in focus group discussion. For instance, the SSO in the R-division explained, 'Since our members took part in "Pantiya", the families and local residents, who had not connected to us, have paid attention to participants' capability of development'.

Weaknesses

The participants and SSOs classified four and three elements of weakness respectively from the narrative data. All SSOs agreed with the idea of the 'decrease and immobilisation of the participants'. One of the SSOs, who worked in the AM-division, said, 'In the beginning phase after the launch of "Pantiya", many disabled people and their families participated in the opportunity. The number of participants, however, decreased gradually'. Another SSO in the AI-division stated, 'Yeah, the regular members tend to be fixed, so that the number of newcomers has been fewer than the early days'. The SSOs noted the issue of 'too much time before results are realised', which means that it takes the time to turn the community workshops into a stable operation.

Disabled people and SSOs also noted the negative aspects of facilities and sources. Participants of community workshops described 'instability of the venue', 'difficulty in the procurement of tools and equipment' and 'lack of operating funds' as weaknesses. For instance, a female in the AM-division (45, physical impairment) said in a focus group discussion:

> *We don't have enough money and tools to manufacture dairy products here. Now, we bring some raw materials which are affordable or free [e.g. banana stems], but we hope to make higher quality products.*

Opportunities

Three and four elements of opportunities were respectively identified from data in the narratives of the participants and SSOs. The 'presence of model activities' is drawn from narrative data from focus group discussion in community workshops in the AM-division and AI-division. A female participant (45, physical impairment) in the AM-division said, 'It was a good opportunity for us to learn how to run our "Pantiya" through visiting R-division. We want to develop our "Pantiya" like R-division'. In the same manner, SSOs mentioned 'accumulated past experiences within the district'. The SSO in the AI-division stated, 'We need to visit R-division again. They have an initiative role in promoting "Pantiya". We can learn various things from their experience'.

With regard to continual operation, disabled people and SSOs noted opportunities to use 'existing techniques' and 'existing resources and collaborators' respectively. A female participant in the R-division (26, intellectual impairment) said, 'Participants usually bring raw materials to "Pantiya" because the materials and tools are insufficient in "Pantiya"'. The SSO in the R-division said:

Although it is difficult for us to procure materials and tools due to a lack of funds, now we can manage to use existing materials such as pieces of clothes, and our techniques. Additionally, many people like other officers support us in holding our "Pantiya".

The SSOs also mentioned 'evaluation of the matter at a national level', because the holding community workshop ('Sthapita karana lada ape iskole vadasatahan sankyaava' on the official report format in Sinhalese) has been officially added as a matter in the monthly progress report by the Department of Social Services at a national level since May 2014. This means that the department has recommended that SSOs in all divisions hold community workshops.

Threats

The participants and SSOs respectively identified one and four elements of threats in the narrative data. They both noted 'poor transport links and accessibility'. The SSO in the AT2-division, where the community workshops have temporarily stopped running, said, 'We face difficulties gathering in one place due to the bad accessibility. So, participants have to spend a long time to come and much money to access "Pantiya". We cannot solve this issue immediately by ourselves'.

SSOs also noted 'lack of understanding by families' and 'secondary effects of disability benefits'. The officers in the R-division and AM-division said that many disabled people and their families tend to stop participating in any activities after receiving disability benefits (Rs. 3,000 per month), which are provided to 50 disabled people in each division. The SSO in the AM-division continued and said, 'Their purpose seems to be only receiving money. Some of the families waste the money by spending it on their family rather than on the disabled person'. These narratives imply the issues, which are barriers to promoting participation in local activities, including community workshops.

'Instability of support by the officers' was noted by SSOs. The SSO in the R-division said, 'It is necessary for our members (disabled people and their families) to take the initiative to run activities such as "Pantiya" and self-help groups. Actually, there is a possibility that the SSOs will transfer to other divisions'.

7.3. Discussion

Using the framework of the SWOT analysis, the results indicate the positive and negative attributes of community workshops, which are one of the model local resources in developmental social work activities in CBR in the Anuradhapura district. This study found strong support for the importance of local resources in the CBR programme from the perspective of disabled people and SSOs (or developmental social workers). The results also show that local people can take full advantage of the opportunities and strengths to overcome the weaknesses of local resources. Therefore, this study contributes to the understanding of the way stakeholders, including disabled people, not only use but also develop local resources.

The most provocative set of findings from this study concerns the relationship between existing local resources, ownership, and sustainability in terms of developing local resources in developmental social work practices. Using existing resources, which is one of the principles of the CBR strategy (Helander et al., 1989; Sharma & Deepak, 2001), incorporating collaborators, local techniques, and physical materials, local people could continually hold community workshops in rural areas where the number of resources such as funds and materials was substantially limited. This study, therefore, suggests the promotion of developing resources by utilising existing resources. In addition, the developmental social work activities using local resources also promoted the feeling of 'our' ('Ape'/අපේ) resources, which can lead to their ownership and sustainability. This perspective corresponds to the principles of CBR guidelines, which state that 'reducing the dependency on human, financial and material resources from external sources will help ensure greater sustainability' (WHO et al., 2010, p.37).

Institutionalisation, such as adding the performance matter to monthly progress reports, and accumulated past experiences, including model practice in other divisions, can encourage the sustainable development of local resources and developmental social work practices. In rural areas where there are no NGOs directly related to the CBR

145

programme, such a cycle of developing resources in a win-win relationship with disabled people and the government sector was essential. In a context similar to that of Sri Lanka, where the government sector manages CBR as a national programme, collaborative activities would be able to have a wide range of effects. Even in a national programme, the results of this study demonstrate the feasibility of community-based developmental social work practices and the potential of promoting the model practice. Therefore, I suggest the combination of multilevel practice based on bottom-up activities, whilst in some cases leveraging the top-down system and administrative power, such as promoting a best practice at a national level (See Chapter 2).

The process of this research indirectly indicates the effectiveness of developing local resources via collaborative activities. In particular, it is fundamental for outsiders, including overseas supporters, to plan, take action, and share their progress with local people in CBR (Peat, 1997; WHO et al., 2010). Using the framework of the SWOT analysis, participatory methods such as focus group discussions, outreach courses, and dialogue in various meetings were effective in involving core stakeholders in grassroots practices.

Previous Publication: This chapter is a revised and expanded version of Higashida, M., Illangasingha, M. G., & Kumara, M. S. (2015). Developing local resources in community-based rehabilitation programme in Sri Lanka: Follow-up study in Anuradhapura. *International Journal of Social Work and Human Services Practice, 3*(1), pp.1-8.

146

CHAPTER EIGHT

Practice 2: Community Mobilisation

This chapter examines community mobilisation from the developmental social work perspective. The WHO (2010) defines community mobilisation as 'the process of bringing together as many stakeholders as possible to raise people's awareness of and demand for a particular programme, to assist in the delivery of resources and services, and to strengthen community participation for sustainability and self-reliance' (p.19). As indicated in Section 1.3., facilitating community mobilisation, including social capital, is expected to associate with developing resources and improving conversion factors in community. The objective of this study is to examine community mobilisation in the R-division, whilst focussing on the impact made by key stakeholders on the socioeconomic participation of disabled people. This study attempted to answer two research questions:

1. *Which factors of developmental social work do promote stakeholders' mobilisation? (Entry and promotional factors.)*

2. *What is the impact of stakeholders' mobilisation on the socioeconomic participation of disabled people? (Impact.)*

After analysing local human resources related to the CBR programme in the R-division, the focus of the study was on volunteers (n = 17), youth club members (n = 7), and local government officers from multiple sectors (n = 33). A semi-structured interview, focus group discussion, and case information provided data, which were collected through social work practice in line with a previously developed one-year action plan. Thematic analysis was applied to the narrative data.

In September 2013, stakeholders of the CBR programme in the division, including the SSO and I, wrote a one-year action plan, which included indicators aimed at challenging the issues that were found out in the previous research (Chapter 6). The logical framework focuses on community mobilisation of the main stakeholders: CBR volunteers, youth club members, local government officers, and local institution staff. Activities with the youth services section were commenced prior to the action plan.

8.1. CBR Volunteers

Entry and promotional factors

Table 17 shows the proportion and main activities of the CBR volunteers, who consisted of four disabled people, five family members, and eight other stakeholders. The CBR volunteers, comprising disabled people and their families, were appointed by SSOs after consulting them. Others were found at the village meetings, such as elderly associations that the SSOs supported as part of their duties, and were appointed as CBR volunteers. The meetings of CBR volunteers were held bimonthly to report the progress of supports and share necessary information in the R-division. Training for CBR volunteers was held once, in 2013, by the SSO and chief SSO in Anuradhapura district.

Reporting on the method of introduction and guidance, the SSO stated:

The new CBR volunteers go to the field with me to find non-registered disabled people because they have more information on disabled people in their living area. Additionally, I recommend holding the CBR village committees to gather disabled people in order to share the community situation and discuss disabled people's needs.

The SSO also recognised the importance of management and capacity building of CBR volunteers 'because they don't tend to work actively alone by themselves'.

All the CBR volunteers reported positive feelings about working with disability issues. The main contents are categorised into three areas: 'As a peer volunteer', 'Happy to make contributions', and 'Religious well-being'. 'As a peer volunteer', interviewee no. 1 stated, 'Because I have spent a long time with them, I enjoy working with them. At the beginning, I felt resistance to support them. But, after being familiar with it, I felt a sense of fulfilment'. He continued, 'I needed somebody's assistance and help in the past, but...now it is possible for me to help someone because I have participated in CBR for many years'. Under the second category ('Happy to make contributions'), all interviewees said that they were satisfied with their activities because they could make a positive contribution. Interviewee no. 5 said, 'I'm very happy to support other disabled people, because they can develop their capability through various activities, although I think more disabled people should take part in such activities'. Finally, regarding 'Religious well-being', interviewee no. 9 stated, 'One of the reasons for working as a volunteer is the action of accumulating many virtuous deeds'.

Table 17: Activities of CBR volunteers in 2013–2014

No.	Age	Sex	Years	Position before CBR Volunteer	Village Committee	Community Workshop	Events	Home Visits
1	25	M	5	DP		✓	✓	✓
2	19	F	2	DP		✓	✓	✓
3	36	M	1	DP	✓	✓	✓	✓
4	61	F	5	DP			✓	✓
5	49	F	1	Family		✓	✓	✓
6	51	F	1	Family		✓	✓	✓
7	56	F	3	Family	✓		✓	✓
8	55	F	15	Family	✓	T		✓
9	61	M	16	Family	✓		✓	A
10	43	F	16	Montessori	✓	✓	✓	A
11	35	F	1	SA	T			✓
12	69	F	16	EA	T			✓
13	61	F	2	EA	T			✓
14	66	F	3	EA	T			✓
15	65	F	1	EA	T			✓
16	60	F	16	Other			✓	A
17	57	F	16	Other	T			✓

Notes: Adapted from Higashida (2014a). ✓ = continually conducted; T = temporarily conducted; A = visited all households in the area; DP = disabled people; SA = Samrudhi association; EA = elderly association; Montessori = teachers in Montessori. Though not an official CBR volunteer, no. 3 is included in the list due to his activities as a 'building relationship officer'.

However, narratives of the interviewees revealed barriers that restrict their commitment to grassroots activities. Amongst the personal reasons given, interviewee no. 10 said that she was required to take care of her mother whose health condition was severe, and interviewee no. 6

stated that she needed to take care of her cows every day. In addition, during the focus group discussion, interviewee no. 12 mentioned, 'Some community people don't show respect to us, so that it is difficult for us to do assertive home visits'.

Impact

Case data registered by CBR volunteers and the SSO are compared by the presence or absence of placement of CBR volunteers. The number of disabled children under 18 years of age, registered in the presence areas (3.22 per 1,000 population), is significantly higher than in the absence areas (1.39 per 1,000 population) in the R-division (p = .04).

Nevertheless, at the focus group discussion, the CBR volunteers placed more importance on other activities. Only one participant (interviewee no. 10) mentioned personal assistance and the home visit programme in the target area to find hidden disabled people. Other volunteers pointed to a higher impact from group and community activities, such as religious events for disabled people, community workshops, and CBR village committees. Interviewee no. 6 said, 'I believe that it is important for us to involve disabled people in many opportunities. Thanks to CBR and our community workshops, our "families" (disabled people) have the chance to go outside, to interact with their friends, and to develop their skills'.

8.2. Youth Club Members

Entry and promotional factors

According to the YSO, she did not have a substantial relationship with social services, including disability issues, prior to 2008. The YSO said, 'The previous SSO didn't recognise disabled people in this division due to the lack of home visits, and I didn't have a chance to collaboratively conduct any activities with them'.

Youth club members started participating in disability-inclusive activities after the present SSO was assigned to the local government office in 2008. About 10 members regularly take part in the inclusive events mainly considered by the SSO and the YSO. The first event held by disabled people and youth club members was the New Year Festival (on the lunar calendar) of disabled people in April 2009. Youth club members participated in the event to support and liven it up.

All interviewees mentioned the change in their attitudes regarding disability issues, whilst being satisfied with inclusive activities. Interviewee no. 1 said, 'I knew some disabled people, but ...I used to consider them as if they were just innocent poor people who were born according to "Karma". (After participation in the CBR programme) I realised that disabled people are also human beings same as us....So, they should have rights same as ordinary people'. Interviewee no. 6 found disabled people were accomplished: 'Now, I realise they are very talented people because they can do various things. Like, some people can sing very well'.

Impact

The members regularly take part in the events for disabled people, such as cultural events and Disabled People's Day Festival (3rd of December), whilst inviting disabled people to the events held by youth clubs, such as sports festivals, leisure camps, and leadership camps. In

2014, for example, 83 disabled youth from three divisions participated in a 3-day camp that the youth club members coordinated in the R-division. In addition, seven disabled youth took part in a Youth Sports Festival in 2013. Moreover, since 2013 one of the interviewee (no. 5) has become an officer of the club through the recommendation of the YSO. Interviewee no. 5 said, 'I am very happy to participate in youth club activities because I can invite my peers (other disabled people) to great opportunities'.

Apart from the change in personal attitudes, the impact of participation of youth club members was also demonstrated. Stating the need for change in the attitudes of other community people, interviewee no. 3 said, 'They have the ability to do something, they have their own skills, we have to identify what their skills are, and they need somebody's help to sharpen their abilities, like CBR volunteer services. And, it is worth it if people like us also give our support too'.

Interviewee no. 1 mentioned the desire to take action in the community in the future by stating, 'I want to be a YSO and to support disabled youth as well as non-disabled youth in the area, in order to empower them. I consider it as a meritorious act'. Interviewee no. 3 stated, 'I want to be a divisional secretary who can develop the community. For example, if accessibility in the community is improved, many disabled people would be able to participate in local activities'.

8.3. Local Government Officers and Local Institution Staff

Entry and promotional factors

Whilst multisector collaborative activities and programmes were limited, some officers had contact with the SSO in the field of coordinating services such as poverty reduction and support for the livelihood of disabled people. The interview with the SSO and other officers revealed that absolutely no collaborative project was implemented before 2008.

The turning point came when the SSO and other members of the R-division's CBR programme began to organise these collaborative projects. Holding meetings to share ideas and giving reasons for the activities were significant developments. Official letters were sometimes required to invite other sectors. Table 18 gives examples of the meetings held to involve stakeholders.

For example, in 2014, when a new project was begun for out-of-school children including disabled children, the conference on child development and CBR played an important role in building a working network with development officers, child-related officers, zonal education officers, and school teachers, amongst others.

At the same time, the involvement of stakeholders in building networks between the social services section and other sectors was fundamental. Involving community stakeholders—such as the midwives at the Medical Officer of Health (MOH), the Grama Niladhari (village officers), and co-medical staff at the community psychiatric unit—was necessary for sharing information, for liaison, and for reference in order to provide accurate support for disabled people and their families.

Impact

In the process of building networks between multisectors, a wide range of programmes has been implemented in the R-division. Firstly, as shown in Table 19, referrals to appropriate sectors were carried out by multisectors. The interview with the SSO did not reveal any cases referred between the social services sector and health and educational sectors, as of 2012. When action was taken on the basis of the one-year plan, the number of referring cases increased in each area. For instance, a person with psychiatric impairment, isolated in the community, was referred to a training opportunity that the local government implemented.

Secondly, the project for promoting educational participation of out-of-school children under 18 (including disabled children) was started. After making plans to collect and integrate information on all villages with the development officers and Grama Niladhari, the survey identified dropout children, including disabled children. The JOCVs have collaboratively implemented home visits to refer the children to appropriate existing resources and to develop alternative local resources.

Thirdly, awareness-raising events were conducted. For instance, disabled people, their families, local government officers, and other stakeholders implemented an awareness-raising demonstration. The aim was to advocate for women's rights, including disabled women in society. The event was publicised in the national newspaper in September 2014 (Figure 13).

Table 18: Multisectoral meetings (examples)

Meeting	Purpose	Stakeholders	Frequency
Child development and CBR	To discuss child issues such as out-of-school pupils, including disabled children	Child- related officers, SSO, officers of the educational sector, Medical Officer of Health, police, overseas volunteers, etc.	Twice a year
CBR progress meeting	To manage progress of the CBR programme based on the action plan	Divisional secretariat, SSO, Samrudhi officers, youth services officer, officers of the educational sector, CBR volunteers, disabled people, etc.	Monthly or bimonthly

Note: Adapted from Higashida (2014a).

Table 19: Referring to other stakeholders

Case Information	Human Resources	Before Intervention	After Intervention
Disabled infants and children under five years old	- Medical Officer of Health (MOH)	N/A	11 cases
Out-of-school pupils including disabled children	- Teachers (two schools) - Development officers/ Grama Niladhari	N/A N/A	9 cases 13 cases
People with a psychiatric impairment	- Officers at a community psychiatric unit (Anuradhapura)	N/A	6 cases

Note: Adapted from Higashida (2014a).

8.4. Discussion

To sum up, this study found strong support for community mobilisation in the CBR programme from the developmental social work perspective. The promotional factors and the impacts of community mobilisation, which are the research questions, are discussed in the following sections.

Entry and Promotional Factors of Community Mobilisation

The opportunities for participation in the CBR programme vary for stakeholders. The analysis reveals, however, the importance of coordination, attitudes, and community-inclusive development for the promotion of community mobilisation. Coordinators to connect stakeholders with the programme and meetings with stakeholders are essential to effectively promote community mobilisation. In this study, the SSO took the main responsibility for managing CBR volunteers and activating a multisector approach. However, there are limitations to be considered. The number of SSOs is limited to only 2–3 in each division in Anuradhapura district.

Attitudes of stakeholders, or the community, are also a fundamental factor in promoting continual participation, which would be considered conversion factors from the viewpoint of disabled people. All CBR volunteers had positive feelings about their work in the programme; however, the type of attitude depended on individual volunteers. Although the youth club members initially felt confused, through mutual participation they had gradually become accustomed to collaborating with disabled people. Interviews with youth club members revealed a change in their attitudes, which led to further participation in disability-inclusive activities.

Finally, multisector practices were implemented, such as the programme for out-of-school children including disabled children. This is one of the examples of disability-inclusive developmental social work to tackle social barriers and to change various conversion factors (See also Section 10.1.). Multisector meetings, including participation of DPOs, are necessary to make decisions and take action related to disability-inclusive development. In addition to promoting dialogue at meetings and with the coordinators, sharing positive achievements and rewards would foster a win-win relationship between all the sectors.

Impact of Community Mobilisation

The analysis reveals that local supporters, including SSOs developmental social workers—and disabled people, make positive contributions to the CBR programme. Using the concept of the 'Twin-Track Approach' (Kuno & Seddon, 2003), which emphasises a simultaneous process of empowerment and inclusion in CBR, the impact on socioeconomic participation of disabled people is divided into two aspects: empowerment and disability-inclusive development.

Firstly, community mobilisation influenced the practice of empowerment and promotion of socioeconomic participation (freedom to participate and achieved participation). For example, CBR volunteers took on the responsibility of identifying disabled people in the community and of promoting socioeconomic participation in local activities under the facilitation of SSOs. In addition, multisectors undertook a supportive role to identify disabled children less than 18 years of age and people with psychiatric impairment, and to refer them to appropriate sectors.

Secondly, mutual support rituals by villagers in the community have developed through the SSO's facilitation in the CBR programme. For instance, by collaborating with the youth services section, mutual participation in youth activities has been developed since 2009. Youth club members have participated in disability-inclusive activities, and disabled youth have taken part in youth club events on a regular basis.

Furthermore, programmes related to inclusive development have been conducted at the grassroots level. One such example is the women's rights awareness-raising event organised by various stakeholders including disabled women and supportive villagers in community. These are considered actions to change the social environment, or conversion factors, in community (See also Section 2.3).

Figure 13. Women's rights awareness-raising event
Note: I obtained the participants' permission to take and use these photos.

Previous Publication: This chapter is a revised version of my article: Higashida, M. (2014). Community mobilisation in a CBR programme in a rural area of Sri Lanka. *Disability, CBR & Inclusive Development, 25*(4), 43-60.

CHAPTER NINE

Practice 3: Integration Of Religion And Spirituality

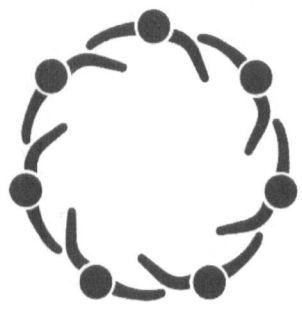

Social exclusion and limited opportunities for disabled people to participate in society, including in religious activities, must be addressed (WHO et al., 2010). However, discussions on indigenous social work practices in non-western cultural societies to address these issues are limited. This chapter focuses on these disability issues and social work practices. I discuss religion and issues pertaining to disability and developmental social work practices (Boxes 7 and 8).

With social work in disability issues, it is significant 'to work with religious leaders and members of all faiths within the community to promote the inclusion of people with disabilities in their activities' (WHO et al., 2010: p. 32). From the perspective of CBID (WHO et al., 2010), inclusiveness in various areas, which consist not only of health, education, and livelihood but also of religion and spirituality (RS), is essential.

Box 7: Moral/Religious Model of Disability in Sri Lankan Context

The moral or religious model, which is a model of disability, considers 'disability as resulting from immorality or sin' (Mackelprang & Salsgiver, 2016, p. 98). For example, religious thought, such as 'Karma' (කර්ම), may have a negative impact on disabled people in Sri Lanka (Liyanage, 2017), because some may consider the association between disability and retribution or 'what goes around [in their previous life] comes around [in this life]' (Miles, 1995). Liyanage (2017) stated, 'Buddhism...doesn't prescribe fatalism and people are not supposed to submit themselves to karma alone...However, in the local social context, disability is seen as an outcome of one's own past actions...' (p.253).

Source: **Higashida (2019a, 2019b)**

Box 8: Basic Terms of Buddhism in Sri Lanka

Buddhist insights that can be brought into spiritually sensitive social work are utilised by some social workers (Canda & Furman, 2010). Although it is beyond the scope of this study to analyse the theory and history of Theravada Buddhism in Sri Lanka (see Kariyawasam, 1995; Perera, 1988; Yong, 2007), a brief explanation of some of the concepts in the religion, which are relevant to this study's analysis and discussion, is provided below.

'**Pin**' (පින) and '**Paw**' (පව්) are important concepts that are utilised in the daily conversations of locals and show a way of life. 'Pin' means merits or good deeds, which believers accumulate through 10 different methods such as, for example, donation ('**Daana**'/දාන). The donation involves donating to marginalised groups such as beggars, orphans, older adults, and disabled people. Ceremonies of '**Pirit**' (පිරිත්) chanting are often followed by another one such as '**Saanghika daana**' (සාංඝික දාන), which is alms given to monks. The opportunity to observe precepts at a temple, called '**Sil samadan weema**' (See Chapter 4), is also an important beneficence for worshippers who, wearing white, gather and listen to monks preaching ('**Bana**'/බණ). In contrast, 'Paw' means demerits, misdeeds, pity, or sin, which Buddhists must avoid in their everyday life. It includes the prohibitions that stem from the five precepts ('**Pas Paw**'/පස් පව්), which consist of killing, theft, sexual misconduct, lying, and intemperance (Kariyawasam, 1995).

Source: Higashida (2016)

Since the RS-related practice does not necessarily associate with economic aspects, some researchers may not include it in development social work. However, I argue that the integration of RS is fundamental for developmental social work, because this appears to be an indigenous and sociocultural practice that is prioritised in the community (See also Chapters 2, 4, and 8).

In particular, the practices to promote participation of disabled people in religious activities has not been sufficiently examined in Sri Lanka, although the literature discusses the negative impacts of religion on disabled people (Liyanage, 2017). Then, I argue that research should also shed light on indigenous strategies to promote disabled people's participation in community.

The objective of this study was to examine the integration of RS into developmental social work practices having to do with disability issues. For this purpose, participant observation with informal interviews with stakeholders was applied in the R-division. [29] The research questions are as follows:

1. *What types of activities are held to facilitate the integration of RS into developmental social work in CBR?*

2. *What are the functions of the integration of RS into developmental social work in CBR?*

---

[29] The main reason for selecting this method is that it is suitable for a participant from the outside trying to understand the construction of social reality (DeWalt & DeWalt, 2002; Flick, 2002). The research period was from February 11, 2013 to January 6, 2015.

9.1. Religion and Spirituality-Related Activities[30]

The RS-related activities were classified into 'daily activities', 'religious activities', and 'private activities' in which mainly primary stakeholders of CBR, such as disabled people, participated. 'Daily activities' were conducted in the CBR programme, including religious observances (Table 20). For instance, at the start of some activities, such as the CBR steering committees and community workshops, participants usually chanted a Buddhist sutra ('Pansil gannawa'/පන්සිල් ගන්නවා) whilst burning incense in front of an image of Buddha. People with intellectual impairments, who had difficulties chanting alone, followed the other participants. In terms of this ritual, the SSO stated,

All members have to participate in 'Pansil gannawa'. Non-disabled people hold the ritual in their everyday life. However, it is very important for disabled people, particularly who spend most of time in their home without any activities and don't have such opportunities.

Perhaps these activities were the integration of RS in daily programmes of disabled people rather than inclusive practice in the community.

---

[30] The findings of this section is based on Higashida (2016).

166

Table 20: RS-related practices in the R-division

Categories	Subcategories	Examples of activities
RS-related activities	Daily activities	'Pansil gannawa'
	Religious activities	'Sil samadan weema', 'Saanghika daana'
	Private activities	Buddhist memorial service, funeral
Secondary RS-related phenomena	CBR volunteers	Home visit, CBR village steering committee
	Youth club members	'Kandawura'
	The others	'Daana'

Note: Adapted from Higashida (2016). RS = religion and spirituality; CBR = community-based rehabilitation.

'Religious activities' in the CBR programme were promoted by the SSO. For example, 'Sil samadan weema' was held on the day close to a full moon day ('Poya'/පෝය), on which many Sinhala Buddhists attend worship at a temple for observances (Figure 14; See Chapter 4), in each month from July 2013 to January 2014. 'Saanghika daana' was carried out after the series of 'Sil samadan weema'. More than 50 members, including disabled people and their family members, many of whom did not attend any usual activities due to household, financial, and physical problems, participated in each 'Sil samadan weema'. One of the disabled people (36 years old) with cerebral palsy said, 'Although I cannot take part in our programme because of the condition of my legs, I am happy to visit a temple with our ('Ape') group members'. The SSO also explained,

Not only spending time at a temple but also
providing opportunities to learn the 'good' and
'bad' things is important for disabled children,
particularly those who don't have experience of
attending school. They don't have opportunities
to gain discretion. It is also good opportunities
for their family members to rethink the way they
bring up their children.

Although this practice also does not involve the inclusion of disabled people into the community's religious activities, due to the integration of special RS activities for them, there are episodes that illustrate the further possibilities. A youth with Down's syndrome (26 years old), for instance, began to visit a temple on a regular basis after the youth and the priest started getting along better as a result of 'Sil samadan weema', including the previous promotion of the priest's understandings of disability issues by the SSO and a CBR volunteer. These daily activities can lead to inclusive religious opportunities.

Trips to places related to Buddhism—namely, the famous temples of Kalutara in 2013 and Kelaniya in 2014 (Figure 15)—were held three times during the research period. Although one of them was subsidised by the Department of Social Services, the rest of the trips were planned and implemented through discussions at the CBR steering committee coordinated by the SSO. More than 80 participants took a trip by two chartered local buses each time at their own expense.

In contrast to the disabled people's position as service consumers and participants, the SSO also promoted activities that the disabled

168

people made contributions to the community. They donated food to older adults at the committee of senior citizens in the Senior Citizen's Day. In addition, they donated sachets, which had been made in their community workshop, to a local hospital. The SSO said, 'Our members can do something to make a contribution to society. We should think of that'.

Some disabled people and their family members, who participated in the CBR programme, invited the members to 'private activities'. For example, the members were invited to a Buddhist memorial service on an anniversary of the host's parent, and a funeral for the host's relatives. When the day was announced to the CBR group members and the SSO, other programmes, such as community workshops and village meetings, were often postponed, whilst the SSO recommended to other members to visit the services. Funerals of disabled children were also held in the R-division during the research period. I participated in the funerals of disabled children twice with the SSO and the CBR members. These kinds of ceremonies are possibly related to everyday community activities, but these can include highly religious aspects such as Buddhist manners.

Figure 14. 'Sil samadan weema' in R-division.

Figure 15. A trip to Kelaniya.

Note: I obtained the participants' permission to take and use these photos.

170

9.2. Secondary Religion and Spirituality-Related Phenomena

The category of the secondary RS-related phenomena consists of 'CBR volunteers', 'youth club members', and 'the others'. All of the episodes are not necessarily RS activities, but these include RS-related phenomena in sociocultural activities that secondary stakeholders of the CBR programme participate in.

'CBR volunteers' are registered as official supporters of disabled people and their families in each village by the SSO. The first CBR volunteer group was organised in the R-division in 1998. A total of 16 volunteers implemented supportive activities, such as visiting disabled people's homes, holding the CBR village steering committee, and supporting events, including religious ones, at the grassroots level during 2 years from 2013 to 2014. As the other study (Chapter 8) has revealed through interviews with CBR volunteers, some of the volunteers were motivated by religious thinking, believing that they accumulated good deeds ('Pin') through various activities. A CBR volunteer (60 years old) stated, 'The happiness I receive through supporting socially vulnerable people is beyond description'.

'Youth club members', who were registered and organised by the YSO, held several social events with the CBR steering committee. For example, disabled children and youth participated in youth camps ('Kandawura'/කඳවුර) held about twice annually, whilst the YSO and SSO collaboratively coordinated their activities. Tamil disabled people from the other province took part in one of the 'Kandawura' held in the R-division in 2014, which led to cultural and religious exchanges. Two months after the 'Kandawura', the CBR members in the R-division visited the province by a chartered bus.

171

A youth club member (22 years old) said,

I believed the effect of 'Karma' and felt they were
'Paw' (pity) until I participated in disabled
people's activities. Like other members, I also
changed my way of thinking. I hope villagers
also change their attitude against disabled
people. Now, I think that disabled people are not
'Paw' (pity).

It, therefore, appears to represent the possibility of an attitude change occurring as a result of interactions and activities with disabled people.

'The others', such as the relatives and neighbours of disabled people, as well as 'CBR volunteers', support the CBR programme, whereby the SSO promoted their participation. With regard to the RS activities, they donated local cuisine ('Daana'), that is to say, curry and rice, to disabled people who worshipped at temples for 'Sil samadan weema' and 'Saanghika daana'. In this case, it can be said that the SSO promoted the stakeholders' participation by including RS-related aspects in the CBR programme.

9.3. Discussion

The present study attempted to examine the integration of RS into developmental social work as the indigenous and sociocultural practice. The goals of this chapter were twofold. The first was to investigate the

172

types of integration of RS into the developmental social work practice. The second was to analyse the functions served by the integration, with regard to developmental social work in the CBR programme at the grassroots level.

First, we found various types of RS-related practices, ranging from individual and group activities to community mobilisation. Whilst the SSO promoted these activities through discussions with disabled people and their family members, RS was integrated into developmental social work in the CBR programme. Second, one of the most interesting aspects concerns a far-reaching function of the integration of RS into developmental social work in the CBR programme, which can be interpreted based on the findings and episodes in the following way: the integration functioned as an alternative education, promotion of participation, and a sense of unity.

As the SSO described, an activity that includes religious aspects is likely to provide an alternative education for disabled children and youth. The activity would provide opportunities for making 'good' and 'bad' things confirm to the religious moral norms that they need to live in the community. It supports the arguments of Canda (2013), who has emphasised the importance of the 'spiritual search for meaning, life purpose, moral ways of relating with the world, including (but not limited to) engagement in religious communities' practices and beliefs' (p. 81).

Perhaps the integration of RS promoted the participation of stakeholders in the CBR programme, which would change the conversion factors in the community. The number of primary and secondary stakeholders who participate in the CBR programme has increased since the commencement of various activities featuring RS practices in 2008, according to the SSO. Although RS-related activities were not the only factors promoting participation in the CBR programme, and even though other aspects, such as the localisation of activities, also contributed, the integration was one of the key triggers of community mobilisation (See also Chapter 8).

The increasing number of participants in the CBR programme is also possibly associated with a sense of unity, which is similar to 'the belief in the unity of all' and 'equality of power' (Mosher, 2010). There is no clear evidence that shows the relationship with RS-related activities in the analysed data, but the word 'Ape' appears to be symbolic, as it has a semantic connection to 'Ekamutu' (එකමුතු), meaning 'united' or 'harmonious'. For example, through participating in 'Sil samadan weema' and singing religious songs on the way to a religious trip, they often utilised these words, although the usage of words is not limited in RS-related activities. It can therefore be argued that the integration of RS into sociocultural and community activities probably boosts the feeling of unity and social capital, and activates developmental social work practices, although it may lead to difficulties distinguishing RS from sociocultural aspects in many cases.

In addition, there is the controversial phenomenon related to the participation of disabled people as contributors in society. The inclusion of disabled people in religious activities may also be associated with preventing their exclusion from religious issues and challenge negative attitudes towards them, such as the views regarding 'Karma'. In terms of analysed cases in this study, some may argue that the episode of disabled people contributing implicates their engagement in the common belief system to gain 'Pin' to offset their 'Paw'. It seems inappropriate to interpret the issue more deeply, given the lack of evidence, the exception

174

being the episode and the narratives of a youth member changing his attitude. Nevertheless, the discussion of this study indicates the importance of promoting an inclusive perspective with respect to RS and sociocultural activities. It includes the importance of challenging the attitudes stakeholders have towards disabled people to overcome the exclusion of disabled people from society.

With regard to overall aspects in developmental social work, it is reasonable to describe the integration of RS into its activities in CBR as reconstructing RS in practice. Most of the types of activities may not necessarily be unique from the perspective of the locals in Sri Lanka. The integrated practice, however, enhanced functions of the CBR programme, widening the range of applications to accommodate the real practice.

Finally, it is important to discuss the issue of awareness of antioppressive action. Developmental social work practitioners must be mindful of antioppressive issues (Morgan et al., 2008) and the effect of long-term conflicts within the country (Yong, 2007). In the case of Sri Lanka, there are areas that have great religious diversity, such as Sinhala Buddhists, Tamil Hindus, Sri Lankan Muslims, and Catholics. Recognising the diversity of religious and ethnic groups, whose model case is the Tamil Sinhala event in the R-division, is essential when they try to integrate RS into their developmental social work practice.

Previous Publication: This chapter is a revised version of my articles: 1) Higashida, M. (2016). Integration of religion and spirituality with social work practice in disability issues: Participant observation in a rural area of Sri Lanka. *SAGE Open, 6*(1), 2) Higashida, M. (2019). Participation of disabled youths in religious activities: Indigenous social work practices in rural Sri Lanka. *Journal of Disability & Religion, 23*(1), pp.90-106.

CHAPTER TEN

Summary And Final Reflections

In this final chapter, several important conclusions are derived from the findings of this book. It integrates the findings of the field research with the theoretical frameworks. After summarising the main findings, implications for developmental social work practices in disability issues are explored. Reflection and limitations in this research project are also discussed.

10.1. Summary and Implications[31]

Summary of the main findings

This paper attempted to examine socioeconomic participation of disabled people in rural Sri Lanka, with the overall purpose being to explore practical strategies to promote their participation from the perspective of developmental social work. The research project revealed the difficulties of socioeconomic participation of disabled people and potential practical strategies in rural Sri Lanka. This section first integrates theoretical frameworks with a summary of the main findings of the field research in accordance with research questions (RQs), followed by implications for policy and practice of CBR in Sri Lanka and other fields.

In the theoretical discussion, I placed Sri Lankan disability issues and CBR in the global context. I discussed the concept of socioeconomic participation and theory of developmental social work using the capability approach. I then argued that the context-specific approach was significant for analysing socioeconomic participation and exploring developmental social work practices at the grassroots level (Chapter 1).

Based on the theoretical discussions and frameworks, the findings and discussions of the field research project were presented. First, three placement areas were analysed in terms of the situation of participation of disabled people (Chapters 4 to 6). Although the limited opportunities for socioeconomic participation of disabled people and poverty were likely to be common themes in these districts, each placement area appeared to have different issues, such as the influences of conflict, or

---

[31] This section is inspired by Higashida (2018a).

differences in CBR progress. The findings showed that those who utilised local resources, including CBR activities, improved their life conditions, whilst revealing many disabled people who had poor access for their socioeconomic participation (corresponding to RQ. 1).

Second, with regard to the factors that have an association with socioeconomic participation, this project found that disabled people living in disadvantaged conditions had lower levels of socioeconomic participation than those living without these disadvantages. In particular, previous educational experiences, household economic conditions, perceived resource information, and accessibility to CBR and key stakeholders were common themes. The dynamics of these factors, including marginalisation of disabled people within the household, were also observed (corresponding to RQ. 2).

Third, practical studies were then examined in one of the areas (Chapters 7 to 9), considering the relationship between policy and practice (Chapter 2). In particular, an indigenous approach, social investment, a comprehensive and multisectoral approach, development of existing local resources, and capacity building were emphasised to realise human rights and to promote the socioeconomic equality of disabled people (corresponding to RQ. 3).

Implications for theory and practice

Beyond the context of a specific country, namely Sri Lanka, these findings have important implications for developmental social work practices in other contexts. They indicate that the theoretical frameworks presented in Chapter 1 would be applicable to frontline workers' practices for addressing disability-related inequalities and limited opportunities for socioeconomic participation. This book, including theoretical frameworks and evidence from field research and practice, identified aspects of the socioeconomic participation of disabled people to which developmental social work could contribute.

In reaction to insufficient discussions on the framework of developmental social work as well as the limited range of data and evidence related to CBR in the literature, this book enables developmental social work practitioners to consider the complex dynamics amongst capabilities, functionings, resources, conversion factors, and other factors, together with an emphasis on the social dimensions of its practice. Developmental social work practitioners need to develop indigenous practices whilst gaining experience through practice and sharing knowledge with stakeholders in line with the local sociocultural context. These practitioners could utilise the proposed frameworks, which have space for diverse practices at the grassroots level. The main points are summarised as follows.

First, social workers and other stakeholders, including disabled people, develop available resources that can be converted into the foundation for a person's capability set and opportunities for socioeconomic participation. Developmental social work does not deny the referral of disabled people in disadvantaged conditions to social welfare allowance and remedy services, but it emphasises the perspective of the social investment. Resources include not only the mobility allowance, physical objects (e.g., assistive devices), and personal support that are necessary for them to participate, but also self-help groups, income-generating activities, and inclusive workplaces that are potential means to participate at the community level. As demonstrated in Chapters 5 to 9, after assessing the community's needs and necessary

179

resources for marginalised disabled people, these resources can be developed by mobilising social capital and building networks at the community level, whilst promoting social investment and funding by government, non-government, and private sectors. Developmental social work therefore creates available resources in collaboration with disabled people and local stakeholders by using the social investment strategy and workers' own knowledge and skills.

Second, by utilising existing and alternative local resources, developmental social work improves the social environment and promotes social change in partnership with disabled people and other stakeholders. This is an engagement tool to tackle negative conversion factors in society for mitigating the impacts on the potential opportunities of the disabled people (Saleeby, 2007; See also Chapter 4). There are many options, ranging from personal support and coordination, such as individual placement and support (IPS) and care management, to more socially dynamic actions, such as lobbying for the improvement of employment policies and raising awareness of discrimination against disabled people (Knapp & Midgley, 2010; See also Chapters 2 and 8). Such multidimensional and multisectoral practice can expand the range of potential functionings or the actual participation opportunities of disabled people (Saleeby, 2007; Veal, King & Marston, 2016).

Third, if disabled people have any difficulties choosing which participation opportunities they value due to any impairments, developmental social workers can provide support for decision-making at the micro level. They can also identify what the person would value and coordinate relationships and resources with stakeholders such as family members of the disabled people (See Chapter 4). In other words, supportive practice for promoting choice and expanding a disabled

180

persons' capability set may be conducted simultaneously. Developmental social workers also consider basic principles such as social justice, human rights, and the strength perspective during such coordination, avoiding prioritising other stakeholders' interests (Knapp & Midgley, 2010; Midgley, 2010; See also Chapters 1, 2 and 4).

Finally, the perspective of agency is emphasised at the stage of achieved participation, including capacity development for leaders who have disabilities and community mobilisation through socioeconomic activities. This stage includes leadership training programmes, capacity development of self-help groups and related committees, and the facilitation of collective and sustainable activities (Knapp & Midgley, 2010; See also Chapters 2, and 5 to 9). These practices by developmental social workers would facilitate individual and collective agency (Box 2) of disabled people and would be additional resources that could be converted into a person's capability set (Veal, King, & Marston, 2016).

10.2. Reflection and Limitations

In this section, I reflect on some challenges faced during the field research. It includes the lack of organised information, my positionality, and difficulties experienced in collaborative practice. I argue that finding the balance between flexibility and organisation was one of the important skills required. In addition, some limitations in the field research and those in theoretical and practical frameworks are discussed.

Self-reflection on interview surveys

During the field studies in each site, first, I collected the essential data, including lists of disabled people, and local resources in each field. I asked the local staff to share the existing data with me, and visited the related institutions such as training centres. Second, I organised a research team that consisted of community volunteers and village officers, thanks to the support of host organisations. Third, I conducted the in-home survey and semi-structured interviews with them, whilst conducting participant observation and practices in some areas at the grassroots level. Finally, I presented the preliminary findings of the project for local stakeholders in meetings in each site, before writing up the final papers.

The process of the field research project, however, was not linear, and flexibility was always required from me in the fields. For instance, I struggled to collect sufficient data at the beginning phase, which was the basis of this research project, because of a lack of organised information at these placement organisations. It took much longer to collect the necessary data than I expected. I came to realise that this was a field reality. Whilst I felt impatience due to the time limitation during the field project, I understood that perseverance and tolerance were necessary. In addition, if I, as an 'outsider', forced them to do something considering my own convenience solely, it might generate a power relationship between us. Therefore, it was essential for me to strike a balance between respecting their style of behaviour, including custom and sense of time, and keeping the overall purpose of the study in my mind.

In terms of my positionality as a newcomer from outside the community, it was a good opportunity to learn about the 'unknown phenomena' from locals. My position and basic purpose were introduced to locals, including the research participants, by the local research supporters. I also introduced myself and explained the aim of the study to locals. Most of the locals appeared to understand my positionality, but I tried to ask them, 'Do you have any questions about me and my research?' Many participants often wanted to ask questions about me and discuss the project in detail, before, during, and after the interviews. These discussions were valuable opportunities to understand their background, needs, and opinions.

Third, a collaborative research approach was unlikely to be sufficient, although I also planned to involve disabled people, such as members of self-help organisations, in this project for inclusion of their voices and opinions. I tried to organise a local research team to conduct the project, but the style was sometimes different from the original proposal. I discussed potential supporters with local government officers before arriving on the placements. Local staff and I organised a small-sized team to conduct the survey in line with local contexts and their opinions. However, I could not include disabled people sufficiently. Due to time limitations and my inadequate skills, I had to do this, but I thought that further collaboration with local stakeholders, including disabled people, would be fundamental to conduct the field project on disability issues.

Challenges in participant observation[32]

With regard to challenges during the participant observation in some fields, I summarised them into two aspects in line with my personal experiences by using my field notes: insider/outsider perspectives and researcher/practitioner positionalities.

Insider and outsider perspectives are well documented in the

---

[32] This is based on Higashida, M. (2017c).

literature of participant observation (e.g., Ergun & Erdemir, 2010; McCurdy & Uldam, 2013). It is necessary for field researchers to reflect on a balance between both the observer's positions, although the extent of emphasising either position would depend on the local context, the purpose of research, and the process of transition.

In my case, reflecting on either perspective was a challenge in the field research, since my awareness and position changed at each stage of the field activities. I was originally based outside of Sri Lanka, where I stayed in a local community and worked with a team of the local government office. At the beginning stage in the first half of 2013, I was likely to be an observer as an outsider because I tried to understand the local contexts and activities. My stance at the time was to participate in any related activity as much as possible, having fresh eyes. These participation opportunities involved not only activities in CBR and disability issues, such as community workshops and disabled people's committees, but also local events and private activities, including religious memorial services. Indeed, I always tried to gather information related to these activities from local residents and CBR stakeholders, whilst asking whether it was possible for me to participate in them. During the participation in these activities, I often asked disabled people and local officers about what I did not know before, asking them 'what is this?' 'when/how did you begin?' and 'what is the reason?' The range of themes was broad from local cuisine to religious practice at temples and interviewee's images of disability. Psychologically, it was highly exciting and vivid for me to realise these unknown things. About 6 months later, however, I felt that I had become familiar with the culture, environment, and local language in the rural community. My position at the time seemed to be that of an insider, whilst staying and working with the locals. On the one hand, experiences in the field widened my view points of religious rituals and cultural customs through participation in a variety of activities. On the other hand, I realised that I had sometimes made assumptions of them without confirming the phenomena again. This means that these phenomena and meanings became self-evident through simplification and interpretation in my mind.

Based on the self-reflection of my subjectivity and inadequate understanding, I started to re-ask questions not only about what I was unaware of but also what I was aware of in some cases. This also involved the potentiality of my misunderstandings of phenomena in the study sites. These issues are related to another category in this case study, namely 'researcher/practitioner positionalities', which I will discuss next.

Due to my double positionality as a social worker and a researcher in Anuradhapura, I also faced dilemmas at the grassroots level. These dilemmas can also be discussed in the context of 'an oxymoron in action' between participation and observation (DeWalt & DeWalt, 2011, pp. 28-29). Although I integrated research activities into a plan of social work practice in Anuradhapura, which was approved by related institutions, I had to distinguish as well as synthesise both of them in line with the contexts. In particular, when I switched the positionality in my mind, the dilemmas between practice and research occurred.

On the one hand, my primary task of social work practice was to promote inclusion and participation of disabled people in the community in cooperation with local stakeholders. On the other hand, exploring local practice through observation was also important. It was not necessarily hard for me to be conscious of my positionality as a researcher at beginning phase because I did not lead any activities. Nevertheless, with the passage of time, the distinction became vague. Because my motivation was conducting social work practice with local stakeholders,

185

my actual activities showed a high priority of practice rather than observation. The ambiguity of double positionality would have advantages such as natural observation in usual contexts. From the perspective of research, however, it might make my sensitive observation weak.

This ambiguous positionality led to challenges of data selection issues. In particular, note-taking was a difficult matter to catch key episodes and narratives of disabled people and stakeholders. For instance, when I focused on social work practice rather than observation, I might have missed note-taking of potentially important episodes. Furthermore, it was impossible to record all phenomena and experiences any time in the field, even though I narrowed my focus on a specific theme. What I could do was, then, to select the phenomena and my experiences which I could recognise, but the selection of them might be affected by my own primary positionality and unconscious interest at the moment. Managing double positionality properly, therefore, was essential for me to keep the research project. This means that being conscious of, or self-reflection on, the double positionality was required in the study. In particular, I had to handle the double positionality by reflecting on the balance between my motivation of practice and observation viewpoint.

Limitations in theoretical and practical frameworks[33]

There are some theoretical and practical limitations to this book. First, some limitations are related to the theoretical assumption of the capability approach. Researchers have argued that the capability approach is too individualistic and it is therefore necessary to consider

---

[33] This section is partly based on Higashida (2018a).

the collective aspects in each concept of the approach (Dubois & Trani, 2009; Trani et al., 2011). Whilst this book touched upon the collective aspects of some concepts, the focus on collectivity would need to be further examined (Veal et al., 2016). In addition, because the capability approach is less likely to provide adequate information on the causes behind each factor, other models—in particular the social model of disability—could strengthen the framework for practice to address social issues (Kuno, 2012).

Second, there are some limitations related to the perspective of developmental social work. For instance, one of the roles of developmental social workers is to improve capabilities for disabled people, including opportunities for socioeconomic participation. However, the real needs and choices of disabled people are diverse. This means that emphasising a specific approach, such as social investment, might not be suitable for some persons in the community. Hence, developmental social workers need to consider how reasonable the adaptation of disabled people to such participation opportunities is, and to consider the power relationship(s) involved.

Finally, the feasibility and usefulness of the application of the capability approach depends on future work. The capability approach uses some terms and concepts that include unique meanings and implications. It is therefore likely to be difficult for strangers to this academic circle to understand the perspective, which might cause some misunderstanding (Kuno, 2012). Therefore, frameworks that are easier for practitioners to understand are required. In addition, the range that the proposed framework of developmental social work practice covers is likely to be broad because the capabilities and functionings relate to various areas. Hence, from the perspective of feasibility and practicality,

187

this framework needs to be more developed in terms of the skills, processes, and activities of developmental social workers (Van Breda, 2015).

10.3. Conclusions

This series of studies are, perhaps, the first to cover the comprehensive features of CBR in rural Sri Lanka from the viewpoint of developmental social work, ranging from situation analysis to implementation and evaluation of practices. Notwithstanding the limitations that each study contained, this book provides a better understanding of the various situations and context-specific practices in CBR and disability issues. These findings suggest that developmental social work practices, including an indigenous approach, social investment, and a multisectoral approach, could address the vicious cycle of inadequate education, poverty, and marginalisation. This book argues that these practices expand the potential opportunities for socioeconomic participation of disabled people and to promote disability-inclusive development in rural Sri Lanka.

The global and local situations are likely to change from day to day. As shown in Chapter 1, global disability issues have developed owing to efforts of multiple stakeholders all over the world. They are attempting to develop new strategies and tools to promote inclusion and empowerment of disabled people in society. I suggest that exploring not only global strategies but also an indigenous approach in developmental social work practices is important in globalised society, as contextualisation is a key concept for practitioners.

Previous Publication

Higashida, M. (2014). Community mobilisation in a CBR programme in a rural area of Sri Lanka. *Disability, CBR & Inclusive Development, 25*(4), pp.43-60.

Higashida, M. (2014). Local resources of disabled people in Sri Lanka: Action research on community-based rehabilitation programme. *Sociology and Anthropology, 2*(4), pp.159-167.

Higashida, M. (2016). Integration of religion and spirituality with social work practice in disability issues: Participant observation in a rural area of Sri Lanka. *SAGE Open, 6*(1).

Higashida, M. (2017a). Integration of developmental social work with community-based rehabilitation: Implications for professional practice. *Kokusai Hoken Iryo (Journal of International Health), 32*(4), pp.271-279.

Higashida, M. (2017b). The relationship between the community participation of disabled youth and socioeconomic factors: Mixed-methods approach in rural Sri Lanka. *Disability & Society, 32*(8), pp.1239-1262.

Higashida, M. (2017c). Dilemmas and challenges in participant observation: Lessons from research on community-based rehabilitation in rural Sri Lanka. *SAGE Research Methods Cases Part 2.*

Higashida, M. (2018a). Developmental social work for promoting the socioeconomic participation of persons with disabilities: An application of the capability approach. *Disability, CBR & Inclusive Development,*

29(2), pp.94-117.

Higashida, M. (2018b). Relationship between the policy and practice of community-based rehabilitation: A case study from Sri Lanka. *Journal of Kyosei Studies, 2*, pp.1-31.

Higashida, M. (2019a). Experiences of disabled people making the transition from vocational training to employment in Sri Lanka: An exploratory study. *Asia Pacific Journal of Social Work and Development.* (in press)

Higashida, M. (2019b). Participation of disabled youths in religious activities: Indigenous social work practices in rural Sri Lanka. *Journal of Disability & Religion, 23*(1), pp.90-106.

Higashida, M., Illangasingha, M. G., & Kumara, M. S. (2015). Developing local resources in community-based rehabilitation programme in Sri Lanka: Follow-up study in Anuradhapura. *International Journal of Social Work and Human Services Practice, 3*(1), pp.1-8.

Higashida, M., Soosai, J., & Robert, J. (2017). The impact of community-based rehabilitation in a post-conflict environment of Sri Lanka. *Disability, CBR & Inclusive Development, 28*(1), pp.93-111.

REFERENCES

Akimoto, T. (2017). The globalization of western-rooted professional social work and exploration of Buddhist social work. In J. Gohori, ed., *From western-rooted professional social work to Buddhist social work: Exploring Buddhist social work*. Tokyo: Gakubunsha, pp.1–41.

Asia Development Bank – ADB. (2005). *Disability brief: Identifying and addressing the needs of disabled people*. Bangkok: ADB.

Association of Women with Disabilities – AKASA. (2011). *Research Report on Women with Disabilities 2010-2011*. Anuradhapura: AKASA. (in Sinhalese)

Attanayake, M.T.R.S. (2016). Challengers of social work education in Sri Lanka. *International Journal of Social Work & Human Services Practice, 4*(5), pp.118-120.

Balabanova, D., McKee, M., & Mills, A. (2011). *Good health at low cost 25 years on. What makes a successful health system?* London: London School of Hygiene and Tropical Medicine.

Barclay, L., McDonald, R., Lentin, P., & Bourke-Taylor, H. (2016). Facilitators and barriers to social and community participation following spinal cord injury. *Australian Occupational Therapy Journal, 63*(1), pp.19-28.

Barker, R.L. (1999). Resources. *The social work dictionary 4th edition*, Washington, D.C.: NASW Press, p.412.

Beaudry, J.S. (2016). Beyond (models of) disability? *Journal of Medicine & Philosophy, 41*(2), pp.210-228.

Bieler, R.B. (2006). The MDGs, disability and inclusive development. *Presentation at the World Congress on Communications for Development*, Rome.

Biggeri, M., Deepak, S., Mauro, V., Trani, J.F., Kumar, J., & Ramasamy, P. (2014). Do community-based rehabilitation programmes promote the participation of persons with disabilities?: A case control study from Mandya District, in India. *Disability & Rehabilitation, 36*(18), pp.1508-1517.

Bogic, M., Njoku, A., & Priebe, S. (2015). Long-term mental health of war-refugees: A systematic literature review. *BMC International Health & Human Rights, 15*(1).

192

Boyce, W. (2000). Adaptation of community based rehabilitation in areas of armed conflict. *Asia Pacific Disability Rehabilitation Journal, 11*(1).

Braithwaite, J., & Mont, D. (2009). Disability and poverty: A survey of World Bank poverty assessments and implications. *ALTER-European Journal of Disability Research/Revue Européenne de Recherche sur le Handicap, 3*(3), pp.219-232.

Brett, J. (2002). The experience of disability from the perspective of parents of children with profound impairment: Is it time for an alternative model of disability?. *Disability & Society, 17*(7), pp.825-843.

Brinkmann, G. (2004). Unpaid CBR work force: Between incentives and exploitation. *Asia Pacific Disability Rehabilitation Journal, 15*(1), pp.90-94.

Brunner, R. (2015). Disability and justice: The capabilities approach in practice. *Disability & Society, 30*(2), pp.310-312.

Burchardt, T. (2004). Capabilities and disability: The capabilities framework and the social model of disability. *Disability & Society, 19*(7), pp.735-751.

Buse, K., Mays, N., & Walt, G. (2012). *Making health policy (2nd ed.).* Berkshire: McGraw-Hill Education.

Campbell, F.K. (2009). Disability, legal mobilisation and the challenges of capacity building in Sri Lanka. In Marshall, C. A., Kendall, E., Banks, M. E., & Gover, R. M. S. (eds.) *Disabilities: Insights from across fields and around the world.* London: Praeger. pp.111-128.

Campbell, F.K. (2011). Geodisability knowledge production and international norms: A Sri Lankan case study. *Third World Quarterly, 32*(8), pp.1455-1474.

Campbell, F.K. (2013). A review of disability law and legal mobilisation in Sri Lanka. *LST Review, Law & Society Trust, 23*(308), pp.1-30.

Campbell, J.C., & Ikegami, N. (1998). *The art of balance in health policy: Maintaining Japan's low-cost, egalitarian system.* Cambridge, UK: Cambridge University Press.

Canda, E.R. (2013). Chronic illness and spiritual transformation. In Saleebey, D. (ed.), *The strengths perspective in social work practice* (6th ed., pp.79-96). Boston, MA: Pearson.

Canda, E.R., & Furman, L.D. (2010). *Spiritual diversity in social work practice: The heart of helping (2nd ed.).* New York, NY: Oxford University Press.

Carr, L., & Darke, P. (2012). The philosophies behind DET: Disability and the disabled people's movement. In: L Carr, P Darke and K. Kuno, (Eds.), *Disability equality training: action for change*. MPH Group: Selangor: 49-85.

Cassim, J.K., Peries, T.H., Jayasinghe, V., & Fonseka, L. (1982). Development councils for participatory urban planning: Colombo, Sri Lanka. *Carnets de l'Enfance* (57-58), pp.157-187.

Cayetano, R.D.A., & Elkins, J. (2016). Community-based rehabilitation services in low and middle-income countries in the Asia-Pacific region: Successes and challenges in the implementation of the CBR matrix. *Disability, CBR & Inclusive Development, 27*(2), pp.112-127.

CEIC. (2018). *Sri Lanka GDP per capita*. Retrieved from https://www.ceicdata.com/en/indicator/sri-lanka/gdp-per-capita [accessed 15 November 2018]

Chandraratna, D. (1991). Alternative models of development: The Sarvodaya experience in Sri Lanka. *Asia Pacific Journal of Social Work & Development, 1*(2), pp.76-90.

Chang, F.H., Coster, W.J., & Helfrich, C.A. (2013). Community participation measures for people with disabilities: A systematic review of content from an international classification of functioning, disability and health perspective. *Archives of Physical Medicine & Rehabilitation, 94*(4), pp.771-781.

Cornielje, H., Majisi, J., & Locoro, V. (2013). Capacity building in CBR: Learning to do CBR. In Musoke, G., & Geiser, P. (eds). *Linking CBR, disability and rehabilitation* (pp.51-57). Koramangala: National Printing Press. Retrieved from http://www.hiproweb.org/uploads/tx_hidrtdocs/CBR_Africa_Final_2013.pdf#page=53 [accessed 15 April 2018]

Cornwall, A. (2008). Unpacking 'Participation': Models, meanings and practices. *Community Development Journal, 43*(3), pp.269-283.

Cornwall, A., & Brock, K. (2005). What do buzzwords do for development policy? A critical look at 'participation', 'empowerment' and 'poverty reduction'. *Third World Quarterly, 26*(7), pp.1043-1060.

Corrigan, P.W., & Ralph, R.O. (2005). Introduction: Recovery as consumer vision and research paradigm. In Ralph, R.O., & Corrigan, P.W. (eds.). *Recovery in mental illness: Broadening our understanding of wellness* (pp.3-17). Washington, DC: American Psychological Association.

Davidson, L. (2005). Recovery, self management and the expert patient: Changing the culture of mental health from a UK perspective. *Journal of Mental*

Health, 14(1), pp.25-35.

Department of Census and Statistics, Sri Lanka – DCS. (2001). *Disabled persons by type of disability, sex, rate per 10,000 population and district.* Retrieved from http://www.statistics.gov.lk/pophousat/PDF/Disability/p11d1%20Disabled%20p ersons%20by%20Sex%20and%20District.pdf [accessed 15 April 2018]

Department of Census and Statistics, Sri Lanka – DCS. (2011). *Sri Lanka census of population and housing 2011.* Colombo: DCS. Retrieved from http://www.statistics.gov.lk/pophousat/cph2011/ [accessed 30 October 2016]

Department of Census and Statistics, Sri Lanka – DCS. (2012). *Census of population and housing of Sri Lanka, 2012.* Retrieved from http://www.statistics.gov.lk/PopHouSat/CPH2011/Pages/ Activities/Reports/FinalReport/FinalReport.pdf [accessed 15 April 2018]

Department of Census and Statistics, Sri Lanka – DCS. (2015). *The spatial distribution of poverty in Sri Lanka.* Colombo: Department of Census and Statistics.

Department of Census and Statistics, Sri Lanka – DCS. (2016). *District official poverty lines.* Retrieved from http://www.statistics.gov.lk/poverty/monthly_poverty/index.htm [accessed 22 May 2018]

Department of Census and Statistics, Sri Lanka – DCS. (2017). *Poverty indicators: Household Income and Expenditure Survey, 2016.* Retrieved from http://www.statistics.gov.lk/poverty/Poverty%20Indicators_2016.pdf [accessed 22 May 2018]

Department of Census and Statistics, Sri Lanka – DCS. (2018). *Sri Lanka labour force survey: Annual report 2017.* Retrieved from http://www.statistics.gov.lk/samplesurvey/LFS_Annual%20Bulletin_2017.pdf [accessed 15 November 2018]

Devapitchai, K. (2010). *Action plan for community-based rehabilitation (CBR) in India: Focus on culture and participation.* Saarbrücken:VDM.

DeWalt, K.M., & DeWalt, B.R. (2002). *Participant observation: A guide for fieldworkers.* Walnut Creek, CA: AltaMira Press.

DeWalt, K. M., & DeWalt, B. R. (2011). *Participant observation: A guide for fieldworkers* (2nd ed.). Walnut Creek, CA: AltaMira Press.

Dubois, J.L., & Trani, J.F. (2009). Extending the capability paradigm to address the complexity of disability. *ALTER-European Journal of Disability Research/Revue Européenne de Recherche sur le Handicap, 3*(3), pp.192-218.

Economic and Social Commission for Asia and the Pacific – ESCAP. (1993). *Asian and Pacific decade of disabled persons, 1993-2002*. New York: United Nations.

Economic and Social Commission for Asia and Pacific – ESCAP. (2011). *Disability at a glance 2010: A profile of 36 countries and areas in Asia and the Pacific*. Bangkok, Thailand: United Nations.

Economic and Social Commission for Asia and the Pacific – ESCAP. (2015). *Disability at a Glance 2015: Strengthening employment prospects for persons with disabilities in Asia and the Pacific*. Bangkok: UNESCAP.

Economic and Social Commission for Asia and the Pacific – ESCAP. (2018). *Beijing Declaration, including the action plan to accelerate the implementation of the Incheon strategy*. Bangkok: UNESCAP.

Eide, A.H. (2006). Impact of community-based rehabilitation programmes: The case of Palestine. *Scandinavian Journal of Disability Research, 8*(4), pp.199-210.

Eide, A.H. (2010). Community-based rehabilitation in post-conflict and emergency situations. In Martz, E. (ed.) *Trauma rehabilitation after war and conflict: Community and individual perspectives* (pp. 97-110). New York: Springer New York.

Elliott, D., & Mayadas, N.S. (2001). Psychosocial approaches, social work and social development. *Social Development Issues, 23*(1), pp.5-13.

Ergun, A., & Erdemir, A. (2010). Negotiating insider and outsider identities in the field: 'Insider' in a foreign land; 'Outsider' in one's own land. *Field Methods, 22*, pp.16-38.

Etiaba, E., Uguru, N., Ebenso, B., Russo, G., Ezumah, N., Uzochukwu, B., & Onwujekwe, O. (2015). Development of oral health policy in Nigeria: An analysis of the role of context, actors and policy process. *BMC Oral Health, 15*:56.

Eyssen, I. C., Steultjens, M. P., Dekker, J., & Terwee, C. B. (2011). A systematic review of instruments assessing participation: Challenges in defining participation. *Archives of Physical Medicine and Rehabilitation, 92*(6), pp.983-997.

Feilzer, M.Y. (2010). Doing mixed methods research pragmatically: Implications for the rediscovery of pragmatism as a research paradigm. *Journal of Mixed Methods Research, 4*(1), pp.6-16.

Filmer, D. (2008). Disability, poverty, and schooling in developing countries: Results from 14 household surveys. *The World Bank Economic Review, 22*(1), pp.141-163.

Finkenflügel, H., Wolffers, I., & Huijsman, R. (2005). The evidence base for community-based rehabilitation: A literature review. *International Journal of Rehabilitation Research, 28*(3), pp.187-201.

Flick, U. (2002). *An introduction to qualitative research (2nd ed.)*. London: SAGE.

Foundation for International Training. (2002). *Sri Lanka Country Study.* Retrieved   from: http://siteresources.worldbank.org/INTSARREGTOPLABSOCPRO/121171411 44074285477/20873622/SriLankaDisability.pdf

Ghobarah, H.A., Huth, P., & Russett, B. (2004). The post-war public health effects of civil conflict. *Social Science & Medicine, 59*(4), pp.869-884.

Goodhand, J., & Lewer, N. (1999). Sri Lanka: NGOs and peace-building in complex political emergencies. *Third World Quarterly, 20*(1), pp.69-87.

Government of Sri Lanka. 2012. *National Action Plan for the Protection and Promotion of Human Rights 2011–2016.* Retrieved from http://www.hractionplan.gov.lk [accessed 1 April 2018]

Gray, M. (2002). Developmental social work: A strengths' praxis for social development. *Social Development Issues, 24*(1), pp.4-14.

Gray, M. (2006). The progress of social development in South Africa. *International Journal of Social Welfare, 15*(s1), pp.S53-S64.

Greene, J.C., Caracelli, V.J., & Graham, W.F. (1989). Toward a conceptual framework for mixed-method evaluation designs. *Educational Evaluation & Policy Analysis, 11*(3), pp.255-274.

Grech, S. (2015). *Disability and poverty in the Global South: Renegotiating development in Guatemala.* Hampshire: Palgrave Macmillan.

Greene, J.C., Caracelli, V.J., & Graham, W.F. (1989). Toward a conceptual framework for mixed-method evaluation designs. *Educational Evaluation & Policy Analysis, 11*(3), pp.255-274.

Guest, G., MacQueen, K.M., & Namey, E.E. (2011). *Applied thematic analysis.* London: Sage.

Haines, A., Kuruvilla, S., & Borchert, M. (2004). Bridging the implementation gap between knowledge and action for health. *Bulletin of the World Health Organization, 82*(10), pp.724-731.

Hartley, S., & Okune, J. (2008). *CBR Policy development and implementation.* Norwich: University of East Anglia.

Helander, E., Mendis, P., & Nelson, G. (1980). *Training the disabled in the community: An experimental manual on rehabilitation and disability prevention for developing countries.* Geneva: WHO.

Helander, E., Mendis, P., Nelson, G., & Goerdt, A. (1989). *Training disabled persons in the community.* Geneva: World Health Organisation.

Herath, C.J. (2014). Evidence of indigenization of social work education in Sri Lanka: Indigenization of social work education in Asia. In Akimoto, T. (ed.). *Internationalization & indigenization of social work education in Asia* (pp.121-182). Tokyo: Japan College of Social Work and Asian and Pacific Association for Social Work Education.

Herath, S.M.K. (2017). Indian Ocean Tsunami and its influence on the resurgence of social work as an academic discipline in Sri Lanka. *European Journal of Social Work, 20*(1), pp.42-53.

Higuchi, M. (2002). *Traditional health practices in Sri Lanka.* Amsterdam: VU University Press.

Hosono, A., Honda, S., Sato, M., & Ono, M. (2011). Inside the black box of capacity development. In Kharas, H., Makino, K., & Jung, W. (eds.). *Catalyzing development: A new vision for aid* (pp.179-201). Washington, DC: Brookings Institution Press.

Husain, F., Anderson, M., Cardozo, B.L., Becknell, K., Blanton, C., Araki, D., & Vithana, E.K. (2011). Prevalence of war-related mental health conditions and association with displacement status in postwar Jaffna District, Sri Lanka. *JAMA, 306*(5), pp.522-531.

International Labour Organization – ILO, United Nations Educational, Scientific and Cultural Organization – UNESCO, & World Health Organization – WHO. (2004). *CBR: A strategy for rehabilitation, equalization of opportunities, poverty reduction and social inclusion of people with disabilities: Joint position paper 2004.* Geneva: WHO.

International Monetary Fund – IMF. (2018). *Report for selected countries and subjects, Sri Lanka.* Retrieved from https://www.imf.org/external/pubs/ft/weo/2018/01/weodata/weorept.aspx? sy=1980&ey=2023&scsm=1&ssd=1&sort=country&ds=.&br=1&c=524&s=NG DP_RPCH,PPPGDP,PPPPC,PCPIPCH,GGXWDG_NGDP&grp=0&a=&pr.x=4 4&pr.y=5 [accessed 15 November 2018]

Inter-agency Working Group on Reproductive Health in Crises. (2010). *Inter-agency field manual on reproductive health in humanitarian settings.* Retrieved from http://www.who.int/reproductivehealth/publications/emergencies/field_manual/e n/ [accessed 30 March 2018]

Johnson, R.B., Onwuegbuzie, A.J., & Turner, L.A. (2007). Toward a definition of mixed methods research. *Journal of Mixed Methods Research, 1*(2), pp.112-133.

Kandasamy, N., Soldatic, K., & Samararatne, D. (2016). Peace, justice and disabled women's advocacy: Tamil women with disabilities in rural post-conflict Sri Lanka. *Medicine, Conflict & Survival, 32*, pp.1-19.

Kariyawasam, A.G.S. (1995). *Buddhist ceremonies and ritual of Sri Lanka.* Retrieved from http://www.buddhanet.net/pdf_file/ceremonies-srilanka6.pdf [accessed 15 April 2017]

Kato, T. (2009). Sri Lanka. In Shinfuku, N., & Asai, K. (eds.). *Mental health care of the world/ Sekai no seishin hokeniryo.* Tokyo: Herusu-Shuppan. (in Japanese)

Kawakita, J. (1967). *Hasso-ho.* Tokyo: Chuo-Koronsha. (in Japanese)

Kayess, R., & French, P. (2008). Out of darkness into light?: Introducing the Convention on the Rights of Persons with Disabilities. *Human Rights Law Review*, pp.1-34.

Keraite, A., Sumathipala, A., Siriwardhana, C., Morgan, C., & Reininghaus, U. (2016). Exposure to conflict and disaster: A national survey on the prevalence of psychotic experiences in Sri Lanka. *Schizophrenia Research, 171*(1), pp.79-85.

Kett, M., Stubbs, S., & Yeo, R. (2005). Disability in conflict and emergency situations: Focus on Tsunami-affected areas. *International Disability and Development Consortium Research Report.* Retrieved from http://www.pacificdisaster.net/pdnadmin/data/original/IDCC_2005_Disability_ conflict.pdf [accessed 30 October 2018]

Klasing, I. (2007). *Disability and social exclusion in rural India.* New Delhi: Rawat Publications.

199

Knapp, J., & Midgley, J. (2010). Developmental social work and people with disabilities. In: Midgley, J., & Conley. A. (eds.). *Social work and social development: Theories and skills for development social work* (pp.87-104). London: Oxford University Press.

Korf, B. (2004). War, livelihoods and vulnerability in Sri Lanka. *Development & Change, 35*(2), pp.275-295.

Kuipers, P., & Hartley, S. (2006). A process for the systematic review of community-based rehabilitation evaluation reports: Formulating evidence for policy and practice. *International Journal of Rehabilitation Research, 29*(1), pp.27-30.

Kuipers, P., Kendall, E., & Hancock, T. (2003). Evaluation of a rural community-based disability service in Queensland, Australia. *Rural & Remote Health, 3*(1), pp.1-10.

Kuipers, P., Wirz, S., & Hartley, S. (2008). Systematic synthesis of community-based rehabilitation (CBR) project evaluation reports for evidence-based policy: A proof-of-concept study. *BMC International Health & Human Rights, 8*(3).

Kumara, M.R.S. (2016). *Inclusion socialization of persons with developmental disabilities through improvement of their vocational and artistic skills*. Tokyo: Third Asia-Pacific CBR Congress.

Kumara, P.H.T., & Gunewardena, D.N.B. (2017). Disability and poverty in Sri Lanka: A household-level analysis. *Sri Lanka Journal of Social Sciences, 40*(1), pp.53-69.

Kuno, K., & Seddon, D. (2003). *Kaihatsu niokeru shogaisha bunya no twin-track approach no jitsugenni mukete (Towards a twin-track approach in the disability sector in development*). Tokyo: JICA. Retrieved from http://jica-ri.jica.go.jp/IFIC_and_JBICI-Studies/jica-ri/publication/archives/jica/kyakuin/pdf/200306_02.pdf (in Japanese) [accessed 1 March 2018]

Kuno, K. (2012). Concepts around disability and disabled people (Chapter 4). In: Carr, L., Darke, P., & Kuno, K. (eds.). *Disability equality training: Action for change* (pp.103-170). Kuala Lumpur: MPH Group Printing.

Kuruppuarachchi, K.A.L.A. & Rajakaruna, R.R. (1999). Psychiatry in Sri Lanka. *The Psychiatrist, 23*(11), pp.686-688.

Lightfoot, E. (2004). Community-based rehabilitation: A rapidly growing method for supporting people with disabilities. *International Social Work, 47*(4), 455-468.

Linder, S.H., & Peters, B.G. (1989). Instruments of government: Perceptions and contexts. *Journal of Public Policy, 9*(1), pp.35-58.

Liyanage, C. (2017). Sociocultural construction of disability in Sri Lanka: Charity to rights-based approach. In Halder, S., & Assaf, L.C. (eds.) *Inclusion, disability and culture: An ethnographic perspective traversing abilities and challenges* (pp. 251-265). Cham: Springer.

Lombard, A. (2008). Social change through integrated social and economic development in South Africa: A social welfare perspective. *Journal of Comparative Social Welfare, 24*(1), pp.23-32.

Lukersmith, S., Hartley, S., Kuipers, P., Madden, R., Llewellyn, G., & Dune, T. (2013). Community-based rehabilitation (CBR) monitoring and evaluation methods and tools: A literature review. *Disability & Rehabilitation, 35*(23), pp.1941-1953.

Mackelprang, R. W., & Salsgiver, R. (2016). *Disability: A diversity model approach in human service practice*. New York: Oxford University Press.

MacLachlan, M., Mannan, H., & McAuliffe, E. (2011). Staff skills not staff types for community-based rehabilitation. *Lancet, 377*(9782), 1988-1989.

Mannan, H., MacLachlan, M., & McAuliffe, E. (2012). The human resources challenge to community based rehabilitation: the need for a scientific, systematic and coordinated global response. *Disability, CBR & Inclusive Development, 23*(4), 6-16.

Marks, D. (1997). Models of disability. *Disability & Rehabilitation, 19*(3), pp.85-91.

Mathie, A., & Cunningham, G. (2003). From clients to citizens: Asset-based community development as a strategy for community-driven development. *Development in Practice, 13*(5), pp.474-486.

Mauro, V., Biggeri, M., Deepak, S., & Trani, J.F. (2014). The effectiveness of community-based rehabilitation programmes: An impact evaluation of a quasi-randomised trial. *Journal of Epidemiology & Community Health, 68*(11), pp.1102-1108.

Mauro, V., Biggeri, M., & Grilli, L. (2015). Does community-based rehabilitation enhance the multidimensional well-being of deprived persons with disabilities?: A multilevel impact evaluation. *World Development, 76*, pp.190-202.

May, P., Hynes, G., McCallion, P., Payne, S., Larkin, P., & McCarron, M. (2014).

Policy analysis: Palliative care in Ireland. *Health Policy, 115*(1), pp.68-74.

McCurdy, P., & Uldam, J. (2013). Connecting participant observation positions: Toward a reflexive framework for studying social movements. *Field Methods, 26*, pp.40-55.

McNay, K., Keith, R., & Penrose, A. (2004). *Bucking the trend: How Sri Lanka has achieved good health at low cost: Challenges and policy lessons for the 21st century.* London: Save the Children.

Meekosha, H. (2011). Decolonising disability: Thinking and acting globally. *Disability & Society, 26*(6), pp.667-682.

Mendis, P. (1995). Education of personnel: The key to successful community-based rehabilitation. In O'Toole, B., & McConkey, R. (eds.) *Innovations in developing countries for people with disabilities* (pp.211-226). Chorley: Lisieux Hall Publications.

Mendis, P. (1997). Act for the Protection of the Rights of Persons with Disabilities in Sri Lanka. *Asia & Pacific Journal on Disability, 1*(1).

Mendis, P. (2016). People with disabilities let down again?: An open letter to the President and Prime Minister. *The Island.* [Newspaper on 29 May 2016]

Mental Health Directorate, Sri Lanka. (2005). *The mental health policy of Sri Lanka: 2005-2015.* Colombo: Mental Health Directorate.

Mertens, D.M., & Hesse-Biber, S. (2012). Triangulation and mixed methods research provocative positions. *Journal of Mixed Methods Research, 6*(2), pp.75-79.

Midgley, J. (1978). Developmental roles for social work in the Third World: The prospect of social planning. *Journal of Social Policy, 7*(2), pp.173-188.

Midgley, J. (1995). *Social development: The developmental perspective in social welfare.* London: Sage.

Midgley, J. (2010). The theory and practice of developmental social work. In Midgley, J., & Conley, A. (eds). *Social work and social development: Theories and skills for developmental social work* (pp.3-29). New York: Oxford University Press.

Midgley, J. (2013). *Social development: Theory and practice.* London: Sage.

Midgley, J. (2017). Introduction. In: Midgley, J., Dahl, E., & Wright, A. C. (eds.). *Social Investment and Social Welfare* (pp.13-32). Edward Elgar Publishing.

Midgley, J., & Conley, A. (2010). *Social work and social development: Theories and skills for developmental social work.* New York: Oxford University Press.

Midgley, J., Hall, A., Hardiman, M., & Narine, D. (1986). *Community participation, social development and the state.* London: Methuen.

Miles, M. (1995). Disability in an Eastern religious context: Historical perspectives. *Disability & Society, 10*(1), pp.49-70.

Miles, M. (2002). Disability in an Eastern religious context: Historical perspectives. *Journal of Religion, Disability & Health, 6*(2), pp.53-76.

Ministry of Finance and Planning. (2005). *Mahinda Chintana: Vision for a new Sri Lanka: A ten year horizon development framework 2006-2016.* Retrieved from: https://www.thegef.org/sites/default/files/ncsa-documents/MahindaChintanaTenYearDevelopmentPlan.pdf [accessed 1 June 2017]

Ministry of Finance and Planning. (2010). *Mahinda Chintana: Vision for the future: The development policy framework.* Retrieved from: https://www.adb.org/sites/default/files/linked-documents/cps-sri-2012-2016-oth-01.pdf [accessed 1 June 2017]

Ministry of Health. (2014). *National guidelines for rehabilitation services in Sri Lanka.* Ministry of Health. (drafted on 4 August 2014)

Ministry of Social Empowerment and Welfare. (2016). *Achievements.* Battaramulla: Ministry of Social Empowerment and Welfare.

Ministry of Social Services – MSS, Sri Lanka. (2012a). *Draft of CBR five year action plan.* Battaramulla: Ministry of Social Services. Retrieved from http://www.socialwelfare.gov.lk/web/images/stories/pdf/cbr_national_plan_draft2.pdf [accessed 1 March 2018]

Ministry of Social Services, Sri Lanka – MSS. (2012b). *Progress report on National Action Plan for the Protection and Promotion of Human Rights 2011–2016.* Battaramulla: MSS.

Ministry of Social Services – MSS, Sri Lanka. (2013). *Performance report 2012.* Battaramulla: Ministry of Social Services.

Ministry of Social Services – MSS, & Ministry of Health. (2013). *National action plan for disability.* (draft document)

Ministry of Social Services and Social Welfare (2008). *Including disability in development through the national community-based rehabilitation (CBR) strategy.* Sri Jayawardenepura Kotte: Ministry of Social Services and Social Welfare.

Minister of Social Services, Welfare and Livestock Development. (2015). *Dina 100 wadasatahana 2015 pagatiya* [Progress of 100-day programme 2015]. Battaramulla: Ministry. (in Sinhalese)

Ministry of Social Welfare. (2003). *Draft national policy on disability for Sri Lanka.* Colombo: Ministry of Social Welfare.

Mitchell, R. (1999). Community-based rehabilitation: The generalized model. *Disability & Rehabilitation, 21*(10-11), pp.459-468.

Mitchell, P.M., Roberts, T.E., Barton, P.M., & Coast, J. (2017). Applications of the capability approach in the health field: A literature review. *Social Indicators Research, 133*(1), pp.345-371.

Mitra, S. (2006). The capability approach and disability. *Journal of Disability Policy Studies, 16*(4), pp.236-247.

Mitra S (2014). Reconciling the capability approach and the ICF: a response. *ALTER-European Journal of Disability Research/Revue Européenne de Recherche sur le Handicap, 8*(1), pp.24-29.

Mitra, S. (2017). *Disability, health and human development.* New York: Springer.

Mitra, S., Findley, P.A. & Sambamoorthi, U. (2009). Health care expenditures of living with a disability: total expenditures, out-of-pocket expenses, and burden, 1996 to 2004. *Archives of Physical Medicine and Rehabilitation, 90*(9), pp.1532-1540.

Morgan, V.J., Berwick, H.E., & Walsh, C.A. (2008). Social work education and spirituality: An undergraduate perspective. *Transformative Dialogues: Teaching and Learning Journal, 2*(2), pp.1-15.

Morris, C. (2009). Measuring participation in childhood disability: How does the capability approach improve our understanding? *Developmental Medicine & Child Neurology, 51*(2), pp.92-94.

Mosher, C. (2010). A holistic paradigm for sustainability: Are social workers experts or partners. *Critical Social Work, 11*, pp.102-121.

Moshiri, E., Rashidian, A., Arab, M., & Khosravi, A. (2016). Using an analytical framework to explain the formation of primary health care in rural Iran in the 1980s. *Archives of Iranian Medicine (AIM), 18*(11), pp.2-8.

Mori, S., Reyes, C.M., & Yamagata, T. (2014). *Poverty reduction of the disabled: Livelihood of persons with disabilities in the Philippines*. London and New York: Routledge.

Moore, M. (2013). Disability, global conflicts and crises. *Disability & Society*, *28*(6), pp.741-743.

Morais, N., & Ahmad, M.M. (2011). NGO-led microfinance: Potentials and challenges in conflict areas. *Journal of International Development*, *23*(5), pp.629-640.

Mousavi, T. (2015). The role of community-based rehabilitation in poverty reduction. *Disability, CBR & Inclusive Development*, *26*(1), pp.125-139.

Myrdal, G. (1970). *The challenge of world poverty. A world anti-poverty programme in outline*. London: Allen Lane Penguin Press.

Nagar, S.B. (2015). *Disability and community based rehabilitation*. Saarbrücken: LAP Lambert.

National Institute of Social Development — NISD. (2017). *Report on the employability of Bachelor of Social Work degree programme*. Sri Jayawardenepura Kotte: School of Social Work. (unpublished)

Noffke, S.E., & Stevenson, R.B. (1995). *Educational action research: Becoming practically critical*. New York: Teachers College Press.

Nussbaum, M.C. (2001). *Women and human development: The capabilities approach*. Cambridge: Cambridge University Press.

O'Leary, Z. (2005). *Researching real-world problems: A guide to methods of inquiry*. London: Sage.

Oliver, M., & Barnes, C. (1998). *Disabled people and social policy: From exclusion to inclusion*. Harlow: Addison Wesley Longman.

Palafox, B. (2011). Good health at low cost revisited: Further insights from China, Costa Rica, Kerala and Sri Lanka 25 years later (Chapter 8). In Balabanova, D., McKee, M., & Mills, A., 2011. *Good health at low cost 25 years on: What makes a successful health system?* (pp.235-267) London: London School of Hygiene and Tropical Medicine.

Patel, L. (2005). *Social welfare and social development in South Africa*. Cape Town: Oxford University Press.

Patel, L., & Hochfeld, T. (2013). Developmental social work in South Africa:

Translating policy into practice. *International Social Work, 56*(5), pp.690-704.

Peat, M. (1997). *Community based rehabilitation.* London: W.B.Saunders.

Peiris-John, R.J., Attanayake, S., Daskon, L., Wickremasinghe, A.R., & Ameratunga, S. (2014). Disability studies in Sri Lanka: Priorities for action. *Disability & Rehabilitation, 36*(20), pp.1742-174.

Pelenc, J., Lompo, M.K., Ballet, J., & Dubois, J.L. (2013). Sustainable human development and the capability approach: Integrating environment, responsibility and collective agency. *Journal of Human Development & Capabilities, 14*(1), pp.77-94.

Perenboom, R.J., & Chorus, A.M. (2003). Measuring participation according to the International Classification of Functioning, Disability and Health (ICF). *Disability & Rehabilitation, 25*(11-12), pp.577-587.

Perera, H.R. (1988). *Buddhism in Sri Lanka: A short history.* Retrieved from http://www.buddhanet.net/pdf_file/bud-srilanka.pdf

Persson, C. (2017). Community-based rehabilitation (CBR) in Uganda: A role for social work? In Gray, M. (ed.). *The handbook of social work and social development in Africa* (pp.156-167). Oxon: Routledge.

Ridde, V. (2008). The problem of the worst-off is dealt with after all other issues: The equity and health policy implementation gap in Burkina Faso. *Social Science & Medicine, 66*(6), pp.1368-1378.

Rannan-Eliya, R.P., & Sikurajapathy, L. (2008). Sri Lanka: 'Good practice' in expanding health care coverage. In Gottret, P., Schieber, G.J., & Waters, H.R. (eds.) *Good practices in health financing: Lessons from reforms in low- and middle-income countries* (pp.311-354). Washington, DC: World Bank.

Ranasinghe, P., Mendis, J., & Hanwella, R. (2011). Community psychiatry service in Sri Lanka: A successful model. *Sri Lanka Journal of Psychiatry, 2*(1), pp.3-5.

Richmond, M.E. (1922). *What is social case work?: An introductory description.* New York: Russell Sage Foundation.

Rifkin, S.B., & Kangare, M. (2002). What is participation? In Hartley, S. (ed.). *Community-based rehabilitation (CBR) as a participatory strategy in Africa.* (pp.37-49) London: University College London.

Robeyns, I. (2005). The capability approach: A theoretical survey. *Journal of Human Development, 6*(1), pp.93-117.

Rohwerder, B. (2013). Intellectual disabilities, violent conflict and humanitarian assistance: Advocacy of the forgotten. *Disability & Society, 28*(6), pp.770-783.

Sabatier, P.A. (1986). Top-down and bottom-up approaches to implementation research: A critical analysis and suggested synthesis. *Journal of Public Policy, 6*(1), pp.21-48.

Saleeby, P.W. (2007). Applications of a capability approach to disability and the international classification of functioning, disability and health (ICF) in social work practice. *Journal of Social Work in Disability & Rehabilitation, 6*(1-2), pp.217-232.

Sarvodaya Suwasetha Sewa Society Ltd. (2016). *Community based rehabilitation (CBR) programme.* Moratuwa: Sarvodaya Suwasetha Sewa Society.

Schneidert, M., Hurst, R., Miller, J., & Üstün, B. (2003). The role of environment in the International Classification of Functioning, Disability and Health (ICF). *Disability & Rehabilitation, 25*(11-12), pp.588-595.

Sen, A. (1992). *Inequality Reexamined.* Cambridge, MA: Harvard University Press.

Sen, A. (1999). *Freedom as development.* Oxford: Oxford University Press.

Sen, A. (2005). Human rights and capabilities. *Journal of Human Development, 6*(2), pp.151-166.

Shahtahmasebi, S., Emerson, E., Berridge, D., & Lancaster, G. (2011). Child disability and the dynamics of family poverty, hardship and financial strain: Evidence from the UK. *Journal of Social Policy, 40*(4), pp.653-673.

Sharma, M., & Deepak, S. (2001). A participatory evaluation of community based rehabilitation programme in North Central Vietnam. *Disability & Rehabilitation, 23*(8), pp.352-358.

Siriwardhana, C., Adikari, A., Pannala, G., Roberts, B., Siribaddana, S., Abas, M., Sumathipala, A., & Stewart, R. (2015). Changes in mental disorder prevalence among conflict-affected populations: A prospective study in Sri Lanka (COMRAID-R). *BMC Psychiatry, 15*(1).

Siriwardhana, C., Adikari, A., Van Bortel, T., McCrone, P., & Sumathipala, A. (2013). An intervention to improve mental health care for conflict-affected forced migrants in low-resource primary care settings: A WHO MhGAP-based pilot study in Sri Lanka (COM-GAP study). *Trials, 14*(1). Retrieved from http://www.trialsjournal.com/content/14/1/423 [accessed 1 November 2017]

Siriwardhana, C., & Wickramage, K. (2014). Conflict, forced displacement and health in Sri Lanka: A review of the research landscape. *Conflict & Health, 8*(1). Retrieved from http://www.conflictandhealth.com/content/8/1/2 [accessed 1 April 2018]

Somasundaram, D. (2010). Collective trauma in the Vanni: A qualitative inquiry into the mental health of the internally displaced due to the civil war in Sri Lanka. *International Journal of Mental Health Systems, 4*(1).

Somasundaram, D., & Sivayokan, S. (2013). Rebuilding community resilience in a post-war context: Developing insight and recommendations: A qualitative study in Northern Sri Lanka. *International Journal of Mental Health Systems, 7*(1).

Sritharan, J., & Sritharan, A. (2014). Post-conflict Sri Lanka: The lack of mental health research and resources among affected populations. *International Journal of Humanities & Social Science, 4*(3), pp.151-156.

Subramaniam, J., Hatta, Z.A., & Vasudevan, G. (2014). Introducing the innovations in social work teaching and practice: A micro experience from the National Institute of Social Development, Sri Lanka. In Raju, N.B., & Hatta, Z.A. (eds.) *Social work education and practice: Scholarship and innovations in the Asia Pacific* (pp.54-71). Brisbane: Primrose Hall.

Sugiman, T. (2006). Theory in the context of collaborative inquiry. *Theory Psychology, 16*, pp.311-325.

Summerfield, D. (2000). War and mental health: A brief overview. *British Medical Journal, 321*, pp.232-235.

Taira, B.R., Cherian, M.N., Yakandawala, H., Kesavan, R., Samarage, S.M., & DeSilva, M. (2010). Survey of emergency and surgical capacity in the conflict-affected regions of Sri Lanka. *World Journal of Surgery, 34*(3), pp.428-432.

Terzi, L. (2005). A capability perspective on impairment, disability and special needs: Towards social justice in education. *School Field, 3*(2), pp.197-223.

Thapa, S.B., & Hauff, E. (2012). Perceived needs, self-reported health and disability among displaced persons during an armed conflict in Nepal. *Social Psychiatry & Psychiatric Epidemiology, 47*(4), pp.589-595.

Trani, J.F., Bakhshi, P., Bellanca, N., Biggeri, M., & Marchetta, F. (2011). Disabilities through the Capability Approach lens: Implications for public policies. *ALTER-European Journal of Disability Research/Revue Européenne de Recherche sur le Handicap, 5*(3), pp.143-157.

United Nations – UN. (2004). *The international year of disabled persons 1981.* Retrieved from http://www.un.org/esa/socdev/enable/disiydp.htm [accessed 15 November 2017]

United Nations – UN. (2006). *Conventions on the right of persons with disabilities and optional protocol.* Retrieved from http://www.un.org/disabilities/documents/convention/convoptprot-e.pdf [accessed 15 April 2018]

United Nations – UN. (2015). *Transforming our world: The 2030 agenda for sustainable development.* Retrieved from https://sustainabledevelopment.un.org/post2015/transformingourworld [accessed 15 April 2018]

United Nations – UN. (2016). *Disability in the SDGs Indicators.* Retrieved from http://www.un.org/disabilities/documents/2016/SDG-disability-indicators-march-2016.pdf [accessed 15 April 2018]

United Nations – UN. (2018). *The UN flagship report on disability and development 2018: Realizing the SDGs by, for and with persons with disabilities.* Retrieved from https://www.un.org/development/desa/disabilities/wp-content/uploads/sites/15/2018/12/UN-Flagship-Report-Disability.pdf [accessed 1 January 2019]

United Nations Children's Fund – UNICEF (2003). *Examples of inclusive education: Sri Lanka.* Kathmandu: UNICEF Regional Office for South Asia.

United Nations Development Programme – UNDP. (2018). Human development indicators, Sri Lanka. Retrieved from http://hdr.undp.org/en/countries/profiles/LKA# [accessed 15 November 2018]

United Nations Educational, Scientific and Cultural Organization – UNESCO. (2018). Education and literacy, Sri Lanka. Retrieved from http://uis.unesco.org/country/LK [accessed 15 November 2018]

United Nations Partnership on the Rights of Persons with Disabilities. (2013). *Towards an inclusive and accessible future for all.* Retrieved from http://www.undp.org/content/undp/en/home/librarypage/poverty-reduction/towards-an-inclusive-and-accessible-future-for-all.html [accessed 15 April 2018]

Uppsala Conflict Data Program. (2016). *Number of deaths: Sri Lanka.* Retrieved from http://ucdp.uu.se/#country/780 [accessed 4 November 2016]

Van Breda, A.D. (2015). Developmental social case work: A process model. *Journal of International Social Work, 18*(3): pp.322-337.

Vanni Rehabilitation Organization for the Differently-Abled - VAROD. (2016). *Pathivugal*. Vavuniya: VAROD.

Vasudevan, V. (2014). Indigenization of field practice in social work education in Sri Lanka. In Akimoto, T. (ed.) *Internationalization & Indigenization of Social Work Education in Asia* (pp.158-182). Tokyo: Japan College of Social Work and Asian and Pacific Association for Social Work education.

Veal, D., King, J., & Marston, G. (2016). Enhancing the social dimension of development: Interconnecting the Capability Approach and applied knowledge of social workers. *International Social Work*, pp.1-13.

Verdonschot, M.M., De Witte, L.P., Reichrath, E., Buntinx, W.H.E., & Curfs, L.M. (2009a). Community participation of people with an intellectual disability: A review of empirical findings. *Journal of Intellectual Disability Research, 53*(4), pp.303-318.

Verdonschot, M.M., De Witte, L.P., Reichrath, E., Buntinx, W.H.E., & Curfs, L.M.G. (2009b). Impact of environmental factors on community participation of persons with an intellectual disability: a systematic review. *Journal of Intellectual Disability Research, 53*(1), pp.54-64.

WageIndicator.org. (2016). *World Bank poverty lines for families in national currencies per month.* Retrieved from http://www.wageindicator.org/main/salary/wages-in-context/world-bank-poverty-lines [accessed 23 May 2016]

Walt, G. (1994). *Health policy: An introduction to process and power.* London: Zed Books.

Walt, G., & Gilson, L. (1994). Reforming the health sector in developing countries: The central role of policy analysis. *Health Policy & Planning, 9*(4), pp.353-370.

Walton, O. (2008). Conflict, peacebuilding and NGO legitimacy: National NGOs in Sri Lanka 1: Analysis. *Conflict, Security & Development, 8*(1), pp.133-167.

Weerasinghe, I. E., & Jayatilake, S. (2015). Development of national disability surveillance system in Sri Lanka. *Online Journal of Public Health Informatics, 7*(1).

Werner, D. (1998). *Nothing about us without us: Developing innovative technologies for, by and with disabled persons.* Palo Alto, CA: Health Wrights.

Women's Bank of Sri Lanka. no date. *The women's bank in Sri Lanka.*

Retrieved from https://www.gdrc.org/icm/inspire/womenbank.html [accessed 10 July 2018]

World Bank. (2014). *World development indicators (Sri Lanka), 2014*. Retrieved from: http://data.worldbank.org/country/sri-lanka [accessed 15 April 2017]

World Bank. (2015). *Global poverty line update.* Retrieved from http://www.worldbank.org/en/topic/poverty/brief/global-poverty-line-faq [accessed 1 March 2016]

World Bank, & World Health Organization – WHO. (2011). *World report on disability.* Geneva: WHO.

World Health Organization – WHO. (1980). *International classification of impairments, disabilities, and handicaps*. Geneva: WHO.

World Health Organization – WHO. (1981). *Disability prevention and rehabilitation: Report of the WHO expert committee on disability prevention and rehabilitation.* Geneva: WHO.

World Health Organization – WHO. (1982). *Community-based rehabilitation: Report of a WHO interregional consultation.* Colombo: WHO. (RHB/IR/82. 1).

World Health Organization – WHO. (2001). *International classification of functioning, disability and health.* Geneva: WHO.

World Health Organization – WHO. (2003). *International Consultation to Review Community-Based Rehabilitation (CBR).* Helinski 25–28 May 2003. Geneva: WHO.

World Health Organization – WHO. (2007). *International classification of functioning, disability and health children and youth version: ICF-CY.* Geneva: WHO.

World Health Organization – WHO. (2010). *Measuring health and disability: Manual for WHO disability assessment schedule (WHODAS 2.0).* Geneva: WHO.

World Health Organization – WHO. (2011a). *Technical appendix A, World report on disability.* Geneva: WHO.

World Health Organization – WHO. (2011b). *Mental health atlas 2011: Sri Lanka.* Retrieved from http://www.who.int/mental_health/evidence/atlas/profiles/lka_mh_profile.pdf?ua =1&ua=1 [accessed 19 April 2018]

World Health Organization – WHO. (2012). *Situation analysis of community-based rehabilitation in the South-East Asia region.* New Delhi: WHO, Regional Office for South- East Asia.

World Health Organization – WHO. (2013a). *Compilation of community-based rehabilitation practices in the WHO South-East Asia region.* New Delhi: WHO, Regional Office for South- East Asia.

World Health Organization – WHO. (2013b). *How to use the ICF: A practical manual for using the International Classification of Functioning, Disability and Health (ICF). Exposure draft for commen*t. Geneva: WHO.

World Health Organization – WHO. (2015). *Community-based rehabilitation indicators manual.* Geneva: WHO.

World Health Organization – WHO., & United Nations Children's Emergency Fund - UNICEF. (1978). *Primary health care: Report of the international conference on primary health care.* Geneva: WHO.

World Health Organization – WHO, United Nations Educational, Scientific and Cultural Organisation - UNESCO, International Labour Organisation – ILO, & International Disability and Development Consortium – IDDC. (2010). *Community-based rehabilitation: CBR guidelines.* Geneva: WHO.

Yong, A. (2007). Buddhism, conflict and violence in modern Sri Lanka. *Mission Studies, 24*(1), pp.165-166.

INDEX

commodities, 12, 15

community mobilisation, 16, 70, 117, 147, 148, 158, 159, 173, 174, 181

Community Rehabilitation Committees (CRCs), 106, 109, 110, 111, 113, 114, 116, 117

community volunteers, 45, 47, 48, 55, 182

community workshops, 56, 63, 69, 121, 123, 124, 133, 134, 135, 138, 140, 141, 142, 143, 144, 145, 152, 166, 169

Community-Based Inclusive Development (CBID), 3, 4, 5, 42, 43, 55, 158, 159, 163

conflict-affected area, 68, 71, 103, 104, 105

context-specific approaches, 62

context-specific practices, 39, 188

Convention on the Rights of Persons with Disabilities (CRPD), 2, 5, 8, 16, 35, 120

conversion factors, 24, 26, 77, 78, 79, 81, 82, 83, 99, 100, 101, 102, 103, 116, 147, 158, 159, 160, 173, 179, 180

coordinators, 158, 159

Cornielje et al., 7

cost-effectiveness, 42

Daana/දාන, 167, 172

daily activities, 166, 167, 168

decision-making, 3, 20, 26, 180

deprivations, 11, 19

development economics, 11

dialogue, 15, 20, 66, 134, 146, 159

disability benefits, 139, 144

disability studies, 2, 11

disability-inclusive systems, 42, 64

disabled people's organisations (DPOs), 45, 47, 49, 52, 61, 116, 117, 159

disabled women's groups, 58

discrimination, 12, 180

Divisional Secretariats (DSs), 32, 67, 69, 121, 136, 157

doings, 11

Down's syndrome, 168

downside risks, 3

dropout, 127, 156

Economic and Social Commission for Asia and the Pacific (ESCAP), 3, 71

education system, 46

educational experience, 82, 84, 92, 99, 100, 178

educational experiences, 82, 84, 92, 99, 100, 178

Ekamutu/එකමුතු, 174

elderly people, 121

employment, 37, 46, 57, 64, 72, 108, 112, 180

empowerment, 2, 8, 19, 20, 32, 42, 47, 53, 56, 60, 61, 62, 64, 114, 116, 117, 131, 159, 188

environmental factors, 9, 12, 15, 101, 127

evidence-based, 37

Finkenflügel et al., 37, 119

freedom to participate, 11, 24, 130, 131, 133

FRIDSRO, 48, 55

functionings, 11, 12, 15, 19, 24, 130, 133, 179, 180, 187

Gandhi, M., 50

global South, 3, 104

global strategies, 3, 188

government-led policy, 49, 59

Grama Niladhari, 47, 97, 99, 155, 156, 157

hardship, 79, 81, 82, 83, 84, 88, 90, 100, 116

health deprivations, 23

health-related policies, 43

human development model, 11

human diversity, 15, 23

human resources, 7, 46, 60, 61, 62, 119, 131, 148

human rights, 2, 5, 8, 20, 23, 178, 181

impairment, 19, 71, 73, 79, 82, 84, 85, 87, 88, 93, 95, 98, 108, 111, 112, 113, 114, 117, 138, 140, 141, 142, 143, 156, 157, 159

impairment/activity-limitation, 79, 82, 84

inclusive development, 3, 4, 50, 63, 159, 160, 188

inclusive education, 124

inclusiveness, 4, 163

India, 17, 29, 37

Indian Ocean earthquake and tsunami, 51, 105

indigenous approach, 40, 60, 178, 188

indigenous knowledge, 49, 54

indigenous social work practices, 162

inequalities, 11, 178

information accessibility, 12

information sharing, 127

International Classification of Functioning, Disability and Health (ICF), 8, 10, 11, 15

National Action Plan for the Protection and Promotion of Human Rights, 53

National Council for Coordinating the Work of Disability Organizations, 52

National Council for Persons with Disabilities, 52

National Housing Development Authority (NHDA), 50

National Institute of Social Development (NISD), 45, 46, 54, 62

National Policy on Disability, 52

Navajeevana, 48

networking, 127

Non-governmental organisations (NGOs), 32, 45, 46, 48, 49, 52, 58, 60, 64, 67, 75, 105, 120, 134, 145

non-linear process, 39, 65

non-western cultural societies, 162

norms, 51, 55, 59, 62, 118, 173

NVivo, 66

occupational activity, 56

Occupational Therapy, 46

out-of-school children, 127, 155, 156, 157, 159

ownership, 145

Pansil gannawa/පන්සිල් ගන්නවා, 166, 167

Pantiya/පංතිය, 56, 58, 124, 125, 126, 130, 131, 134, 139, 140, 141, 142, 143, 144

Papissa/පාපිස්ස, 140

participant observation, 66, 165, 182, 183, 184

paternalism, 26

Paw/පව්, 172, 174

Peat, M., 46, 104, 119, 120, 131, 146

peer-supporter, 85, 86, 150

personal assistance, 78, 87, 93, 94, 95, 101, 102, 131, 152

personal factors, 9, 127

physical environments, 19

Physiotherapy, 46, 110

Pin/පිං, 171, 174

policy triangle, 45

political contexts, 6, 7, 71, 104

potential opportunities, 11, 180, 188

poverty, 3, 5, 10, 11, 20, 23, 31, 47, 51, 72, 75, 77, 79, 81, 101, 116, 136, 155, 177, 188

power relationships, 26

Poya/පෝය, 167

www.ingramcontent.com/pod-product-compliance
Lightning Source LLC
Chambersburg PA
CBHW061349280526
45784CB00001B/192

* 9 7 8 0 3 5 9 4 9 8 6 8 0 *